PILATES

WALTER McKONE

BARNES
&NOBLE
BOOKS
NEW YORK

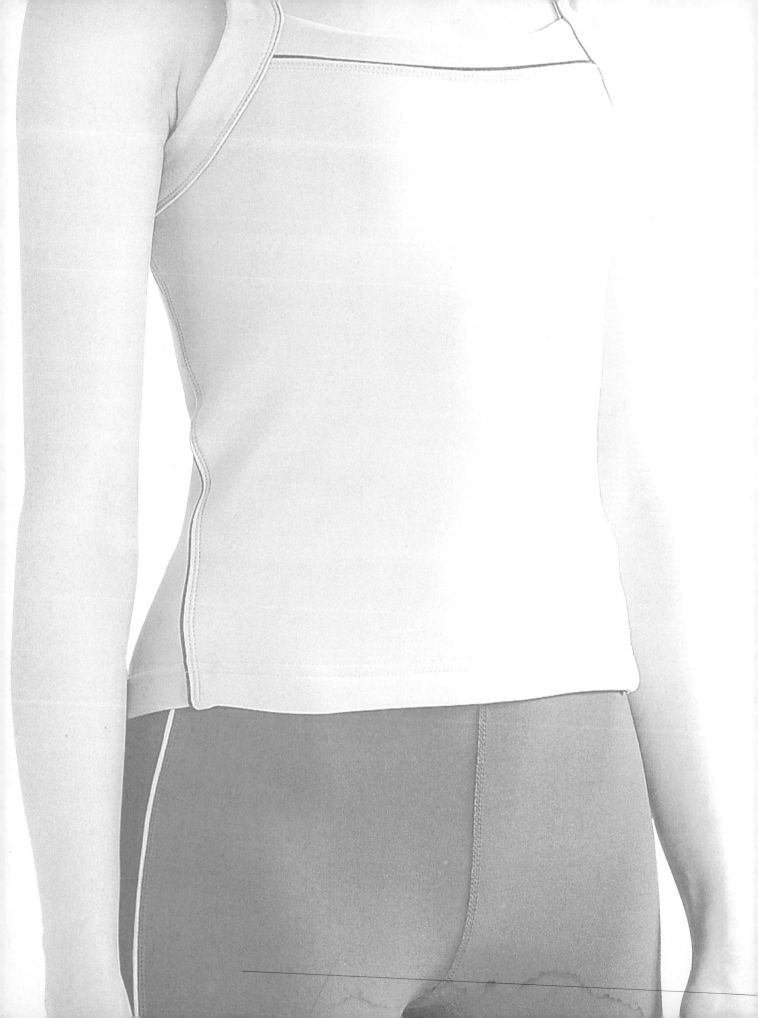

an introduction to
PILATES

Walter McKone

This edition published by Barnes & Noble Inc.,
by arrangement with Parragon

2002 Barnes & Noble Books

M 1 0 9 8 7 6 5 4 3 2 1

ISBN: 0-7607-3136-5

Manufactured in China

Contents

introduction   6

who can use this **Book**?   8

before you **Start**   10

practicing **Safely**   12

how does **Pilates work**?   14

the fascia and muscle **Systems**   16

posture and **Body type**   18

postural **Conditions**   20

body **Type**   22

principles of **Good practice**   24

coordinated **Movement**   26

breathing and **Centering**   28

alignment and **Stamina**   30

introduction to the **Exercises**   32

the **Exercises**   34–89

glossary   90

useful addresses and **Contacts**   92

index   93

acknowledgments   96

introduction

The Pilates approach offers you a gentle but powerful pathway to achieving your natural potential for health, strength, flexibility, and stamina . Developed in the early 20th century, this unique and increasingly popular form of exercise can help you to develop supple movements and strength as well as improve your posture and general well-being.

The Pilates approach combines working on the body's muscle groups with maintaining smooth, flowing movements, a strong, centered posture, breath control, and clear mental focus. The system was developed by Joseph H. Pilates in the early 20th century. A German by birth, he had been a sickly child but used physical exercise to improve his health and physique. He moved to England in 1912, taking advantage of his strength and fitness to become a boxer. However, when World War I broke out, he found himself interned on the Isle of Wight because of his nationality. Pilates passed his time by teaching other internees how to develop their physical fitness. His interest in fitness led him to

The Pilates exercises taught today may differ from those created by Joseph Pilates, but they still adhere to the basic principles of focusing the mind and relaxing and stabilizing the body while you exercise. Pilates principles are as relevant today as they were in the last century.

develop his first piece of exercise equipment. This was the so-called "Universal Reformer," made from the springs of a hospital bed and used to help patients work out as they lay in bed. Pilates found that spinal-injury patients recovered more quickly when they used his equipment and this stimulated his lifelong interest in remedial exercise.

MIND AND BODY

After the war, Pilates moved to the United States and opened a fitness center in New York. His classes became particularly popular with dancers, who identified with his emphasis on flowing movement and mental focus. Pilates continued to develop his system throughout his lifetime, looking to different sports as well as yoga and the animal world to increase his instinctive understanding of the body. In addition, he adapted his exercises to the needs of individual students. Since his death, his students have developed the practice further and there is no one set way of teaching Pilates. However, an intentional mind-body interaction is one of the basic keys to the Pilates approach, wherever it is taught.

PILATES MOVEMENT

neck and shoulders
free from tension

back straight but relaxed

strong abdomen

centred pelvis

Practicing Pilates regularly will help
you to develop core stability and
strength. This increases your
movement control and helps you to
retain a relaxed but strong posture.

weight centered on the feet to
provide a solid foundation

who can use this **Book?**

The Pilates approach to exercise can be used by almost anyone and there is no age starting point or limit. Since the exercises are gentle, any strain on the body is at a minimum. This reduces the risks of injury during and after exercising. Pilates movements reach deep into the body, stimulating good muscle development and a more effective circulation.

Because it encourages you to work slowly and at your own pace, almost anyone can practice Pilates. Most people begin with simple exercises and build up to more advanced techniques, depending on their fitness levels and ability. You can also incorporate the Pilates approach into everyday activities and other forms of exercise.

The exercises in this book are relatively simple and are aimed at providing an introduction to Pilates for people who have reasonable health and are injury-free (see page 11). Practiced correctly and regularly, these exercises can help you to improve your physical and mental well-being in various ways. For example, if you write, use a computer, or drive for long periods, your muscles are likely to tire and, in turn, your posture will suffer. The exercises will help you to strengthen muscle and tissue tone, to give you better support and stability.

USING THIS BOOK

Although this is a practical book, it is recommended that you read it through before trying the exercises. This will help you to understand the fundamental elements of Pilates and vital safety points, which will help you to do the exercises correctly.

Do the exercises a few at a time so that you assimilate the Pilates approach slowly and methodically. Don't try to do too many exercises at once as your focus and efficiency will be reduced if you get tired. Practice two to three times a week if you can. If possible, start with 10 minutes of Pilates in the morning and 10 minutes in the evening and gradually increase the time as you develop.

This book is not intended as a substitute for taking classes with a Pilates trainer, who can help you understand the principles more fully.

You can take up Pilates at any stage of life, although you should start with gentle exercises and build up the time that you spend exercising slowly. Keeping your mental focus will make sure you remain aware of how your body feels, which will help you to exercise safely.

WHAT PILATES CAN DO FOR YOU	
Better flexibility	Pilates helps you to develop flexibility, which improves the range of your movements and the shock-absorbing efficiency of your body. Over time, your movement patterns will become more fluid, allowing you to move with less effort and more grace.
Improved strength	Your strength will increase as the stability of your muscles and joints improves and you learn how to move and use your body more effectively.
Increased muscle tone	Stretching in the Pilates way enhances the tone of your muscles. This gives you support and control even when you are at rest. Good muscle tone is important to provide the body with good structural support at all times. Pilates also avoids ungainly muscle growth.
Improves your circulation	The coordination of slow movements and breathing improves your circulation to particular parts of the body. Different Pilates exercises work specifically to stimulate the circulation to areas of the body that are under your control. Better circulation improves general health.
Deeper, more efficient breathing	One of the essential elements of Pilates is improving your breathing. Better breathing improves oxygen supply and helps to remove carbon dioxide build-up from your muscles.
Greater oxygen supply to blood and all of the body's systems	As a consequence of better breathing, oxygen is more efficiently transported to all of the body's systems by the circulation system. This helps the muscles to work more effectively and thereby increases stamina as well as long-term muscle health.
Reduced stress	Stress reduction is a major benefit of Pilates. Overtension of muscles increases stress, while stretching with breathing enhances greater relaxation.
Improved digestion	The stomach and the intestines are muscles. Pilates helps to tone and relax these muscles, bringing them into their optimum state. This in turn improves the digestive processes that go on within them. In addition, because Pilates helps to reduce stress, overproduction of stomach acids becomes less likely, which reduces the risk of ulcers and other such stomach problems.
Clearer skin	As your circulation becomes more efficient, you improve the body's ability to clear toxins from the skin. In this way, practicing Pilates can lead to a clearer skin.
Trimmer waist, flatter stomach, and more toned buttocks and thighs	The steadily controlled movements in Pilates work the muscles slowly and thoroughly. As mentioned above, this leads to better tone. A more efficient muscle burns body fat more quickly, especially around the areas of the waist and hips.
Stimulates the immune system	A stronger, more relaxed body encourages a good immune system. This is because the circulation of lymph (fluid carrying white blood cells) relies on good muscle movement to pump it around the body. Improved circulation will add to the effect.

before you Start

Self-help books like this one mean that you can take control of your own fitness and decide when and where to exercise. However, this also means that you don't have a teacher to help you make sure that you practice carefully and so you will need to take full responsibility for your own safety.

I t is not difficult to practice Pilates at home but you need to consider various safety factors before you start. Think about the following aspects of your health and situation:

• Practice environment
• Present age and general state of health
• Pregnancy
• Minor illnesses
• Good practice

THE ENVIRONMENT

The environment in which to practice is often overlooked as a factor that can promote or retard the effectiveness of any exercise system. In particular, it is important that you are in a warm area so you don't get cold and tense up your body. However, do not practice in direct sunlight, either outside or in front of a window, or close to a radiator or electric fire, which will heat your body up artificially. In addition, make sure that your practice area has good ventilation and is free from any drafts.

WARNING

The exercises in this book are presented on the assumption that the reader has no previous medical condition. If there is any doubt about your health, seek professional medical advice. The publishers and author cannot be responsible for injury, either in the short or long term.

You are more likely to injure yourself if you exercise when you are cold, so it is essential that you warm up before you start your Pilates practice. One of the best ways of doing this is by going for a short, brisk walk outside or by walking on the spot for a few minutes.

PRESENT AGE AND HEALTH

With regards to your present age and health, it is important to take advice from a medical professional or qualified Pilates trainer before practicing if you answer "yes" to any of the following questions:

• Are you very young or old? Generally, Pilates is safe for people of all ages, but it is safer to check if you are at either end of the spectrum.

• Do you have diabetes?

• Do you have a history of heart or lung conditions?

• Are you on any medication that could put you at risk while exercising?

• If you are postmenopausal, do you have aches or pains that could indicate lack of bone density?

• Do you have any inflammations or swelling in muscles and/or joints?

• Do you have any disease or injury that makes your muscles and/or joints unstable? These include arthritis, torn ligaments, or dislocations.

• Are your periods accompanied by severe pain? You may be at risk when you are menstruating. In general, you should not practice Pilates if you are

You don't need any special equipment to do Pilates at home, but make sure that you practice in a clear, comfortable space. Lie on a rug, carpet, or folded towel to help to keep yourself warm.

suffering from any severe menstrual symptoms, such as back pain, headaches, or weakness. None of these conditions are absolute disqualifying factors and may simply mean that you need to avoid doing certain exercises that might aggravate the ailment.

PREGNANCY

Pregnancy is not a illness. As long as you feel well, can still move around easily, and the bump is not in the way, there is no reason to stop or even start practicing Pilates techniques. If you have any doubts, seek medical advice before you start.

MINOR ILLNESSES

Do not attempt to work off any minor illness with Pilates. This is especially important in cases of viral chest, throat, influenza, and glandular infections, which affect your muscular system. Make sure you have been free from these for at least two weeks.

practicing **Safely**

Spend a few moments checking how you are feeling before, during, and after practicing Pilates. This will help to make sure that you meet your body's needs and that your exercise program is both effective and safe. It will also help to increase your general body awareness, which is an important part of the Pilates approach. Do not force your body past it capabilities.

Pilates is intended to improve your physical and mental well-being, so it is important to make sure that you feel good while you are practicing and that you support your well-being before and after practice. As you develop your practice, you may find that you naturally begin to incorporate better body awareness and activity into your everyday life. In addition, these are some recommendations to use as a checklist.

GOOD PRACTICE

Safe practice should be divided into:
• Prepractice preparation and daily activity
• Practice
• Postpractice

PREPRACTICE

• In general, you should make sure that you are well hydrated—drink at least nine cups of water a day slowly. However, don't drink a large quantity of liquid just before a Pilates session.
• Do not start the practice session if you are in a state of tension. If you are feeling stressed, try walking on the spot to release tension from your body before you begin.
• Be careful if you are too cold. Go for a walk or move gently on the spot to warm up.
• Do not warm up artificially before exercise, for example by sitting in a hot bath, having a shower, or sitting in front of a heater. This can increase the potential for injury.
• Clear your practice area and make sure that you have enough space to stretch out fully during the exercises without knocking into anything.
• Make sure the floor surface is warm—use a mat, rug, or folded towel to practice on.

Drinking enough water is an essential part of healthy living as water helps the body to clear out toxins. How much you drink will depend on how much you are exercising and what the weather is like, but on average, you should try to drink at least nine cups of water each day.

PRACTICE

• Take your time with the speed of the exercise and the number of exercises you do in one session. Build it up slowly and at your own pace.

• Remember, there will be a gentle increase in the strain on your system. For these changes to be beneficial, you must not push yourself too hard.

• Some exercises will seem very gentle while you are doing them and you may not feel their effects until a day or two later. Give yourself a week before returning to exercises like this. This lets body adaptation to take place.

POSTPRACTICE

• Do not just sit down or stop moving after you finish your exercise session. Take a gentle walk or move into some gentle activity, such as taking a shower and getting dressed.

• Do not go straight to bed after going through these exercises in the evening.

Going for a short walk after a Pilates session will help you to manage a smooth transition back to your normal activity. Enjoy your enhanced body awareness and notice if you are holding yourself slightly differently.

Respect your body and don't try to do too much too quickly—even if an exercise seems very gentle. You may not feel the effects until later and your body will benefit most if you build up your program gradually.

How does **Pilates work?**

Pilates exercising is known for its ability to redefine the shape of people's bodies, sculpting them into a naturally optimum form. The reason that it does this so well is because it is such an efficient form of physical exercise and works on different levels of the physical body, including the nervous system, the muscular system, the fascia system, and the skeletal system.

There are four major areas of the body on which Pilates actually works and affects your body. These are:
- The nervous system
- The muscular system
- The fascia system
- The skeletal system.

THE NERVOUS SYSTEM

The nervous system is vital for the control and coordination of movement. It is divided into the central and peripheral systems. The central system includes the brain and spinal cord, while the peripheral system consists of the nerves that course throughout the body. These peripheral nerves deliver messages to the body from the central system and relay messages from the far reaches of the body back. This is how the body "speaks" and provides feedback to the brain. Pilates brings greater awareness of the nervous system and helps you to develop a better sense of how your limbs, muscles, and internal organs feel. In turn, this helps you to find the centered point between tension and relaxation, one of the foundations of Pilates practice.

THE MUSCULAR SYSTEM

Not many people are aware that good and effective muscle contraction begins from a state of relaxation. Achieving a state of relaxation before movement produces more power and control. It also means that

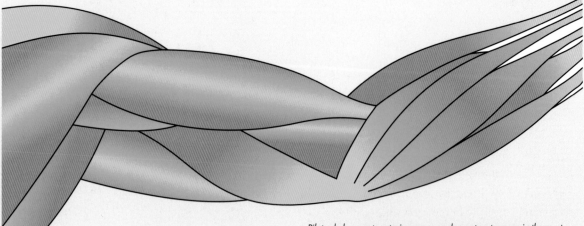

Pilates helps you to retrain your muscular system to move in the most effective way. If your muscles are used to being tense or flaccid, this may take time to achieve. However, the more you bring your muscles back to optimum relaxation, the more comfortable they become in this state.

there is less risk of injury and less pressure on your joints when you move. With a more relaxed and toned muscle system, you are more stable and will burn fat more efficiently. This leads to good body tone, a flatter abdomen, and tighter buttocks. Muscle contraction begins from three positions:
• Optimum relaxation
• Overcontraction
• Overstretching.

OPTIMUM RELAXATION

This is what we are trying to achieve in Pilates. Optimum relaxation is where the muscles and tendons rest with a tension that is full and comfortable. You can only burn off fat if your fat burning tissues (muscles) are efficient. Optimum relaxation makes for the most efficient movement. Animals demonstrate this when they run—the movement is relaxed and fluid.

OVERCONTRACTION

This is when the muscle, with its tendon, does not let go even when you stop moving. Many people have overcontracted shoulders, for example, which remain tight when they try to relax. An overcontracted muscle pulls the joint toward the side of the contraction. This means that when you move, you are not starting from the neutral position and will suffer a slight loss of power. Continued movement from an overcontracted starting point could increase the wear and tear on a joint. If your back muscles are overcontracted, you increase the risk of injury and your central stability is disturbed.

OVERSTRETCHING

Overstretched muscles around a joint can lead to serious instability. If the muscle tone is flaccid and weak, reflex reactions will be slow and the risk of injury will be increased. Sudden recurring strains and sprains, especially in the back, knees, and shoulders, are generally due to this type of underlying problem. In addition, an overstretched muscle will not be able to burn fat effectively.

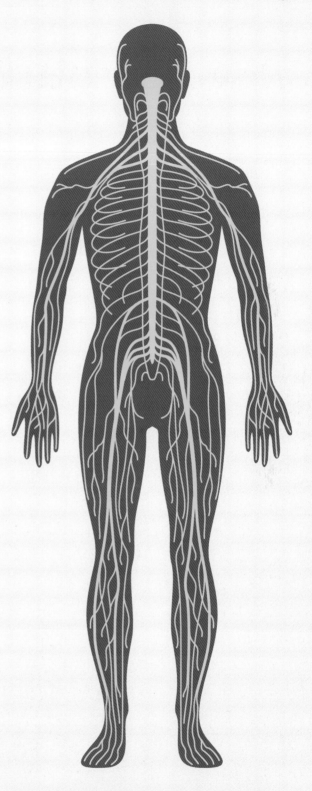

Thousands of nerves run all over the body, carrying messages to and from the brain. Pilates helps you to develop better body awareness. In other words, it helps you to pay more attention to those messages and adjust your position and movements accordingly.

the fascia and skeletal **Systems**

A regular practice of Pilates will help you to develop a stable support for the skeletal system through both the muscles and the fascia (soft tissue) system. All work in tandem to improve your posture and alignment, and, thus, the way you move. However, because bad postural habits will have developed over many years, it will take time to correct them.

An efficient muscular system will improve your strength and support. However, it is also essential to provide strong support through the skeletal and fascia systems, both of which are strengthened by Pilates.

THE FASCIA SYSTEM

Fascia is essentially a packaging tissue. Together with the muscles, tendons, and ligaments, it provides stability and support for the entire body. Unlike the other soft tissues, it is not broken up into separate pieces. Imagine, for example, that the body is a

house: in each room is a muscle with its tendon. In this room is a joint that is formed by two bones and surrounded by a ligament. The bones pass out of the room to form joints in other rooms surrounded by ligaments, muscle, and tendons. The fascia forms the walls, floors, and ceilings of the house, connecting each room with the next. Without the fascia there would be no stability for the muscle, tendons, joints, and bones to move. Pilates exercises work to improve the tone of the fascia, albeit very slowly. Therefore, over time, it makes its own deep and long-lasting contribution to the central stability of the body.

THE SKELETAL SYSTEM

The bone and joint system lies within the muscle, tendon, and fascia systems. It provides a central pivot for the contraction and control of these three soft tissues. In return, these three systems give strength to the bones and their joints, supporting the main joint stabilizers, the ligaments.

The strength of the skeletal structure (bones and joints) is directed by the actions of muscles, tendons, and fascia. The Pilates approach recognizes this as well as the role played by the bones and joints in the fight against gravity, which becomes more difficult as we get older. Adopting a Pilates approach helps to realign the skeletal system and also contributes to the reduced risk of early-onset osteoporosis. This is due to good, centered stability, which allows you to continue almost any form of exercise in later life.

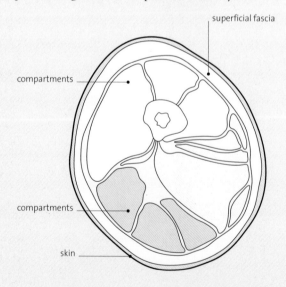

superficial fascia

compartments

compartments

skin

Here you can see how the bone (in this case, the femur) is surrounded by fascia compartments and a layer of fascia that lies just under the skin. The fascia provides protection and stability for the joint and will be gradually strengthened by regular Pilates practice.

THE SKELETAL SYSTEM

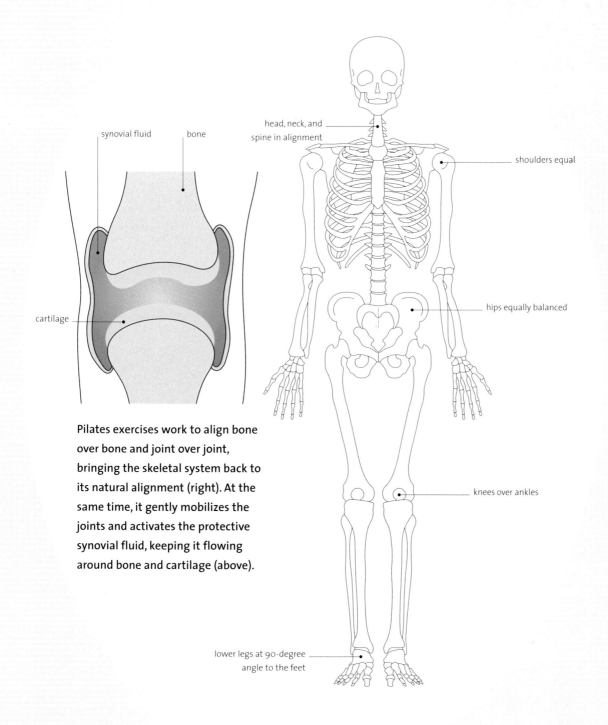

synovial fluid

bone

cartilage

head, neck, and
spine in alignment

shoulders equal

hips equally balanced

knees over ankles

lower legs at 90-degree
angle to the feet

Pilates exercises work to align bone over bone and joint over joint, bringing the skeletal system back to its natural alignment (right). At the same time, it gently mobilizes the joints and activates the protective synovial fluid, keeping it flowing around bone and cartilage (above).

posture and **Body type**

Posture is the starting point of all movement. If your posture is under strain, every movement you make will be inefficient, which leads to tiredness, weakness, and aching muscles and joints. This is why you begin every Pilates exercise by adopting a good posture and relaxing into it and also why you need to incorporate good posture into your daily life.

Posture is the way in which you stand, sit, or lie. You should be able to relax in whatever posture you have adopted and still maintain good muscle tone. If you relax and your posture collapses, then this is an indication that you need to work on your body's stability, for example, by practicing the Pilates exercises.

GOOD POSTURE

You can check your standing posture quite easily if you stand facing a mirror and scan down your body. The following are signs of good posture:
• Level ear lobes
• Level shoulders
• Equal distance between the ears and shoulders
• Equal spaces between arms and body
• Level hips
• Level left and right kneecaps
• Equal shape and contour in your calf muscles
• Equal arches of the feet.
Let yourself relax. If you feel a strain on your neck, back, hips, or legs, then your posture is under strain.

COLLAPSING POSTURE

It is from the side that distorted posture is classified into its six major groups. These are:
• Cervical lordosis
• Thoracic kyphosis
• Thoracic straight spine
• Lumbar lordosis
• Swayback
• Visceroptosis.
It is quite common for some postures to combine some different elements of these conditions.

CERVICAL LORDOSIS

In this posture, the neck spine has moved too far backward and the vertebrae too far forward. As the back of the head and the upper back get closer together, the chin points forward. The muscles at the back of the neck shorten and those at the front become overstretched and tight. At the same time, the vertebrae move forward, stretching and weakening the ligaments at the front of the spine. Joints at the back of the spine suffer compression, which increases wear and tear. Arthritis and other forms of joint inflammation may develop as a result of cervical lordosis, as well as neck pain and stiffness.

THORACIC KYPHOSIS

In the kyphosis posture, the upper back gives the impression that the person is falling forward. As the forward movement progresses, the muscles at the back of the spine stretch and weaken, and the muscles at the front shorten and weaken. Under this pressure, the vertebrae become distorted, the breastbone drops, and the chest becomes compressed. This decreases the efficiency of the lungs and heart. The stomach and intestines also become compressed, which can lead to digestion problems.

CHECK YOUR POSTURE

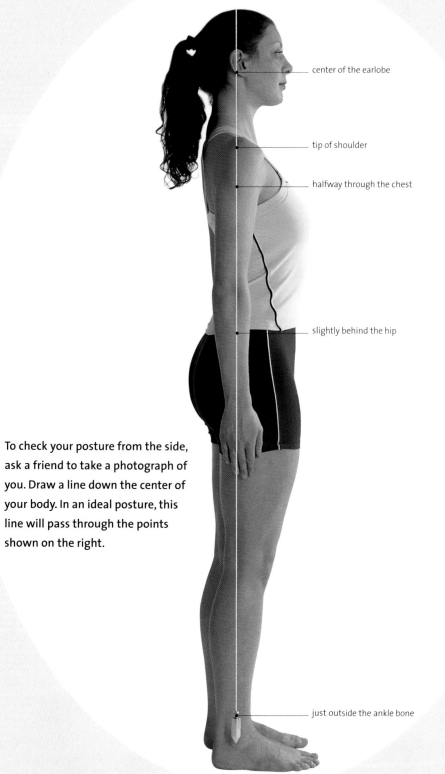

center of the earlobe

tip of shoulder

halfway through the chest

slightly behind the hip

just outside the ankle bone

To check your posture from the side, ask a friend to take a photograph of you. Draw a line down the center of your body. In an ideal posture, this line will pass through the points shown on the right.

postural **Conditions**

Together with those described on the previous page, these are the most common postural distortions. It can be helpful to recognize your particular postural condition so that you can bring your attention to areas of concern as you do the exercises. You may also be able to choose techniques that specifically work to realign areas affected by your posture.

Few people maintain perfect posture into their adult lives. Many of us will suffer from one or other of these spinal postural problems or those described on the previous page.

THORACIC STRAIGHT SPINE
This is a condition where the thoracic spine becomes straight as a result of the shortening of the muscles on the back of the spine. As they contract, the spine straightens, leading to compression of nerves and a disturbance of the ribs. People who suffer from this condition may feel pain and tingling in the arms. In addition, the chest, heart, and lungs come under pressure, which reduces their efficiency.

LUMBAR LORDOSIS
In an exaggerated lumbar lordosis, the vertebrae of the low back are moving forward, giving the appearance that the person is falling backward. It increases pressure on the back of the vertebrae, leading to weakness and pain in the lower back. The abdominal muscles will weaken and the stomach will be dragged forward with the intestines. This disturbs digestion as the circulation to the digestion tract becomes overstretched.

SWAYBACK
The swayback posture is a more overall disturbance than the other postural conditions described. Beginning with a backward tipping of the head, it is

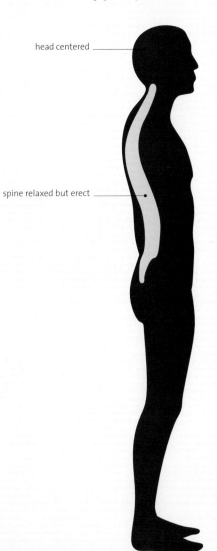

head centered

spine relaxed but erect

This picture shows the natural curvature of a healthy spine. It arches gently inward in the lower back region, outward in the upper back, and inward again in the neck region. Constantly standing or sitting badly leads to a gradual distortion of these natural curves, as shown opposite.

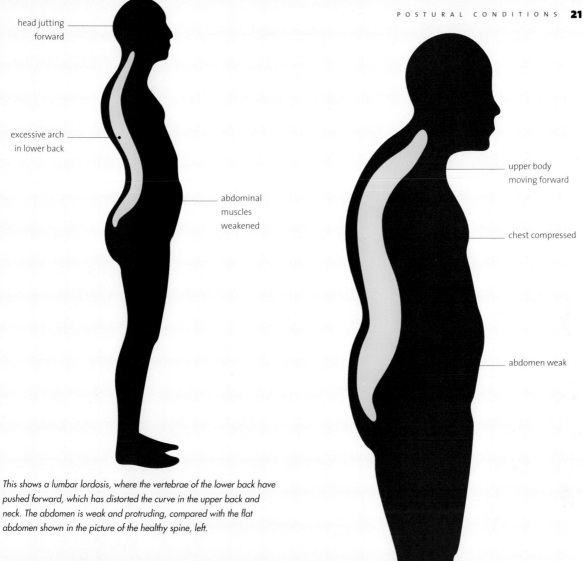

head jutting
forward

excessive arch
in lower back

abdominal
muscles
weakened

This shows a lumbar lordosis, where the vertebrae of the lower back have pushed forward, which has distorted the curve in the upper back and neck. The abdomen is weak and protruding, compared with the flat abdomen shown in the picture of the healthy spine, left.

a long distortion that begins in the thoracic spine, moving down into the lumbar spine, and creating what seems to be a backward pushing of the knees. This is essentially a weakness of the ligaments in the body. Poor muscle tone adds to the problem and there is generally a poor control of movement. Joints, particularly the elbow, may appear double-jointed.

VISCEROPTOSIS

This is the loss of abdominal muscle tone and includes the "beer belly" and bloating on the lower bowel and pelvis. The intestines, kidneys, and womb are dragged downward, overstretching tissues and reducing circulatory and nutritional supply. This precipitates such conditions as period pain, incontinence, and irritable bowel syndrome.

upper body
moving forward

chest compressed

abdomen weak

In this kyphosis, you can clearly see how the spine pushes the body forward, compressing the chest and abdomen and causing the chin to jut forward. This pressure gradually changes the shape of the vertebrae, which become wedge-shaped rather than block-shaped.

body **Type**

Many people are attracted to this form of exercise because of its ability to redefine and tone the body. However, Pilates is all about working within your limitations and it will help you to reach your optimum shape only within the confines of your natural body type.

ECTOMORPH

You may notice that your body starts to change quite rapidly when you begin to practice Pilates—simply learning to hold yourself correctly and relax into good posture can make an immediate difference to the way that you look. Over time, as we have seen, muscle tone improves, improving weight loss, bones and joints can move back into alignment, and overall posture gradually returns to its naturally erect state. However, it is important to realize that Pilates can help you only to make the most of your natural build.

BODY TYPES

Our body types are usually defined according to the dominance of our three body cavities. These cavities are the head, chest, and tummy regions. The body is usually categorized into three forms:
• Ectomorph
• Mesomorph
• Endomorph

These basic body-type descriptions were formulated by the American psychologist William Sheldon. Most of us find ourselves falling between two of these basic types, combining different aspects of both.

The ectomorph is tall and thin with a delicate build and long, thin limbs. Ectomorphs have stooped shoulders and are lightly muscled. They have trouble gaining weight. The mesomorph has a hard, muscular body and is rectangular in overall

The ectomorph is typically a tall, thin person with long fingers and thin wrists. Ectomorphs tend to be very flexible but can still have tight or weak muscles. They have a young appearance and have large brains.

MESOMORPH

appearance. Mesomorphs have an upright posture, thick skin, and develop muscle quickly. Endomorphs have a generally round shape with underdeveloped muscles and a prominent chest and stomach. They tend to have trouble losing weight.

ENDOMORPH

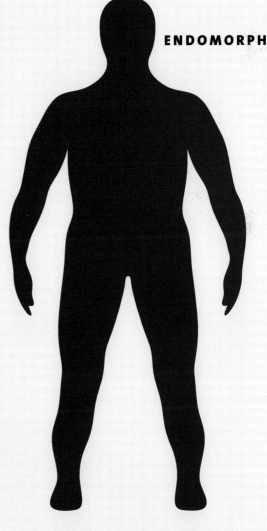

A mesomorph is usually athletic in his or her appearance, with large arms and legs, large chest, and a tight tummy region. Mesomorphs have good muscle development and are often good at sport.

Endomorphic people appear shorter and squatter than the ectomorph or mesomorph types. They are generally thick necked with a round shape. Their movements tend to be short and tight and they have a large chest region. They have trouble developing muscle and losing weight.

principles of **Good practice**

The Pilates approach involves far more than simply exercising your muscles. Learning to concentrate your mind and let go of held tension from the body before you move are two vital elements that help to make the Pilates practice a whole body-mind experience. The other main elements of good practice are discussed on the following pages.

Joseph Pilates had a natural understanding of how a mind-body dynamic could be used to achieve whole health, and taught his students how to incorporate mental focus into their practice.

This is part of what makes Pilates a unique form of exercise. All Pilates practice should incorporate the following principles:
• Mental focus
• Relaxation
• Smooth movements
• Good coordination
• Controlled breathing
• Body centering
• Body alignment
• Stamina

MENTAL FOCUS

Pilates is a total mind-body program and you need to approach each exercise with good mental focus in order to feel its full benefit. By concentrating on how and where you are moving, you are more likely to move in the correct way. In addition, as you bring your thoughts to your

By incorporating good mental focus into your exercises, you will be more likely to retain a stable, centered posture and practice the exercises correctly and safely.

movements, you will become more adept at interpreting your body sensations. These provide you with useful feedback and help you to judge more easily the correct state of tension or relaxation for each position or movement.

Practicing mental focus while you are doing Pilates will help you to improve your body awareness in general, enabling you to become more in tune with the physical sensations of your body and the messages that they can give you in daily life. When you begin practicing Pilates, all of your attention may be focused on coordinating the movement. As you become more familiar with the exercises, you can use your mind to focus on more subtle aspects of the process. In any case, keep your focus light. If you concentrate too hard, you will lose awareness or frustration may set in. If you do start to feel tired or tense, take a short break to help relax your mind. This brings us to the second fundamental principle of Pilates, relaxation.

RELAXATION

Because most of us hold tension in our bodies, we rarely reach a state of complete relaxation. For this reason, it is helpful to see relaxation as an activity that has to be practiced rather than something that

A relaxed body posture is essential in all Pilates exercises. However, Pilates relaxation does not mean simply letting go of all muscular tension, but also requires you to stand, sit, or lie in a way that provides good stabilization and support for your body.

you do naturally. Everyone holds their tension in different areas of their body; the way to find your particular areas of tension is to sit or lie down comfortably and focus systematically on the different parts of your body.

Imagine that you are floating in water and that your body is completely supported. What parts of your body are resisting your wish to let go? Start at your toes and slowly work your way up your legs, through your body, and to your head, then go down to your fingertips, and work your way up your arms and shoulders to your head again. As you do this, let go of the tension in each area in turn, breathing deeply and feeling it start to relax. You may not find it easy to do this at first but don't try too hard or for too long or you will become tired.

You can practice this when you are sitting or standing as well as lying down. Try doing it on the bus or in your car (at the lights). Eventually, you'll be able to maintain a sense of relaxation in movement. It is when you achieve this that you will get maximum benefit from the Pilates exercises.

coordinated **Movement**

Smooth, coordinated movements are a crucial aspect of the Pilates approach. Jerky or fast actions mean that you have lost your mental focus and make physical injury or muscle strain more likely to occur. Learning to move in a slow and gentle way helps you to respect your body and use it to reach your potential. It also makes the body more efficient and effective.

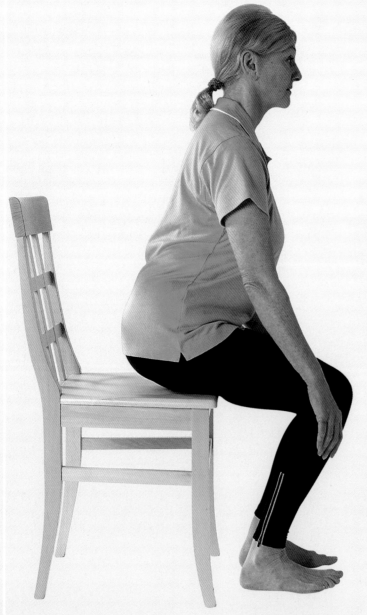

P racticing good movement technique will help you to perform Pilates exercises safely and effectively. The more you incorporate smooth movement into your exercises, the more automatic it will become. Eventually, you will find that you start to use your body in a healthier, more relaxed way throughout the day.

SMOOTH MOVEMENTS

Have you ever watched a wildlife program where the film speed has been altered to show a zebra, tiger, or other animal running in slow motion? What immediately draws your attention is the fluidity of the movement that takes place. Animals, unlike most humans, are relaxed when they move, which is why their actions are so efficient and graceful. When you move from a point of tension, the action is less efficient so you use more energy and tire more quickly and may pull your body out of alignment.

It takes time to learn a more gentle and graceful approach to movement. This is one of the reasons why Pilates exercises are performed slowly, giving the body time to assimilate the movement, and why they have a cumulative rather than instant effect.

In everyday life, most of us rush about in a state of tension. Watch how people move around in the street or at work and notice how jerky most of their

Try to bring smooth and flowing Pilates movements into simple daily actions, such as sitting down or standing up, as well as into the exercises themselves.

movements are. Using tense, jerky movements leads to higher energy use, which in turn places greater demand on the internal organs, such as the heart, liver, and kidneys. Smoother movements reduce the demand on the internal organs, which helps them to function to the best of their ability. Thus, practicing Pilates helps to strengthen the relationship between our internal organs and our muscle system.

If you use flowing movements throughout life, you are much less likely to injure or strain your body. This is true not only for exercise and sporting activities, such as tennis, football, or golf, but also in everyday activities, such as picking things up, gardening, or driving. To practice and develop flowing movements, try to relax your body before and as you move, releasing physical tension and concentrating on keeping a good sense of balance.

COORDINATION

Smooth movements rely on good coordination of the different muscles and joints. Some Pilates exercises, such as the Backstroke (see pages 60–61) and Light Arms and Strong Legs (see pages 42–43), specifically coordinate different movements to help develop this natural skill.

In Pilates, movements are also coordinated with the breath (see page 28). This can feel difficult to begin with—rather like learning new dance steps—but having good mental focus helps. At first, your attention is focused on each movement and breath, then gradually, the sequence starts to flow until the coordination comes to you automatically.

Practicing coordinated movements regularly means that, over time, the body becomes used to performing them with ease. Eventually, this sense of ease will be incorporated into all your daily activities.

breathing and **Centering**

Breathing correctly and centering your body are two of the most crucial aspects of performing Pilates. They form the essential foundation of all the exercises. Smooth breathing will help you to move more efficiently and maintain your energy levels while maintaining a strong physical center means that you use your body in the most effective, safe, and balanced way.

Good breathing and a strong center are essential for all the exercises. Holding your breath while you are moving causes the body to tense, while losing your center throws your body out of its alignment and weakens your support.

BREATHING

Breathing is the essence of life and promotes good health when it is performed in a relaxed manner. Most of us breathe shallowly, into the upper chest, or we may have learned to practice abdominal

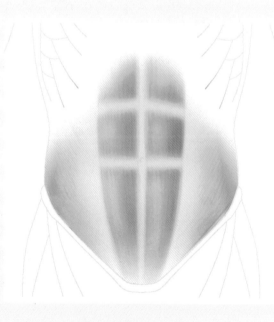

Maintaining good tension in the abdominal region means that you contract the transversus abdominis, the main stabilizing muscle for the center of your body, stabilize all movement, and support your spine.

breathing, to promote relaxation and reduce stress. Neither of these breathing methods is suitable for Pilates. In Pilates, we try to use our lungs and chest capacity to the fullest, while maintaining good muscle tone in the abdomen for support (see below). The best way to breathe efficiently while you exercise is to draw the air into your back and the sides of your ribcage, making use of your full lung and chest capacity. This is called thoracic or lateral breathing. The more oxygen that you get into your lungs, the more oxygen-rich blood is delivered to your muscles and organs, helping them to work efficiently, effectively, and for longer.

In the Pilates approach, your breath is synchronized with your movements. It is important to follow the directions for the exercises precisely as each action is specifically linked to either an in or an out breath. This ensures the proper use of the muscle groups and reduces any tendency to hold your breath. When you hold your breath, you start to store up more carbon dioxide in your lungs. This does not get completely expelled from the body with the out breath. Instead, it builds up in the muscles, especially the core muscles, and weakens them. Keeping up a good breathing rhythm when you perform the exercises promotes good oxygen-carbon dioxide exchange.

In addition, the physical movement of lateral breathing is a mechanical action that helps to pump blood around the body. Thus, while you work your

A good guide to the amount of muscle tension to use is to reach a point about halfway to what you feel is tight and then relax a little more below that level. Do not force your body beyond its limits.

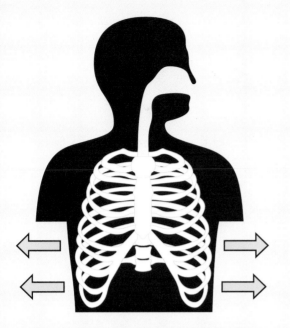

In Pilates, you breathe into your back and the sides of your lower ribs. This helps you to bring the maximum amount of oxygen into your body, which promotes effective working of muscles and internal organs.

chest movements, you are moving all the fluids around your body at the same time, helping to take nutrition to your body tissues.

CENTERING

Joseph Pilates realized that bringing strength to the abdominal area gave support and stability to the entire body. This is because a tight, firm abdominal region brings a core of stability to the middle of your body, which helps to stabilize your every movement and support your spine. This central stability is supplied by a large, deep, flat muscle, which is known as the transversus abdominis. One of the best ways to bring support to the middle area is to pull gently back on the abdominal muscles, moving your navel closer toward your spine. This also helps to protect and support your lower back. At the same time, increase the tone in the pelvic floor by gently pulling up on it.

Maintaining this light muscle tension while you are breathing out creates stability of the central part of your body. However, you do not want to use too much abdominal muscle tension to bring the navel toward the spine or to lift up the pelvic floor.

You can use a scarf wrapped around your lower ribs to help you learn the art of lateral breathing. Go to page 52 for more detailed instructions on how to do this. It can take a few weeks of practice to get right.

alignment and **Stamina**

Bringing your body back into its perfect alignment may be a long process but most people see subtle changes to the way they hold their body quite quickly once they start practicing the Pilates techniques. Holding your body in an efficient way combines with good breathing to provide you with the stamina to hold your position for longer.

All Pilates exercises work to improve your alignment, but it's important to go only as far as your body comfortably can. If you push it further, you will move out of line.

ALIGNMENT

When you incorporate the basic elements of Pilates into your exercise, you encourage your body to find its natural alignment. This means your most efficient posture in standing, sitting, and lying positions. As your muscles begin to balance themselves, there will be less stress placed on your joints, and your internal organs will work with greater ease.

All your muscles and joints will work more efficiently and there will be less wear and tear on the joints. Mechanically, you move with less resistance when you are in proper alignment and this means your actions will place less stress on your heart and lungs. In addition, good alignment reduces the risk of ligament and joint injury while participating in athletic and sporting activities.

Combining your Pilates practice with a form of anaerobic or aerobic exercise is an ideal way to achieve optimum health. Try cycling, swimming, or some other form of vigorous exercise that you enjoy.

STAMINA

Due to the slow nature of the Pilates approach the heart or cardiovascular system does not really achieve a good workout. You build up stamina through increasing your deep breathing capability rather than your heart function. Most Pilates instructors recommend that you also participate in anaerobic and/or aerobic exercises, such as running, tennis, or walking, to support your Pilates exercises. As your breathing becomes more effective, you will exchange oxygen and remove carbon dioxide more efficiently from your muscles, which reduces fatigue. This helps you build up the stamina to hold postures, which makes for a solid base on which to begin and hold all movements.

NATURAL ALIGNMENT

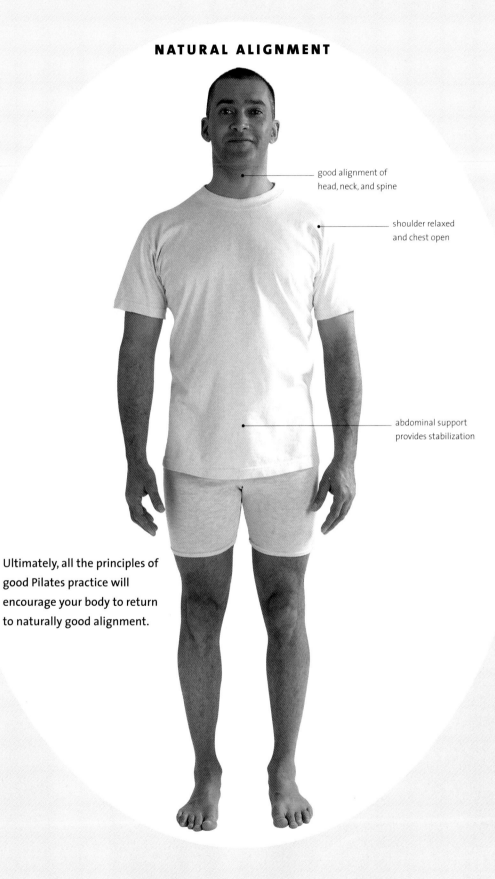

good alignment of
head, neck, and spine

shoulder relaxed
and chest open

abdominal support
provides stabilization

Ultimately, all the principles of
good Pilates practice will
encourage your body to return
to naturally good alignment.

introduction to the **Exercises**

The exercises in this book are intended to provide a gentle but effective introduction to the Pilates technique. They are not intended as remedial exercises unless you have sought medical advice. Each exercise works on different muscle groups but incorporates all the basic principles of the Pilates approach, such as breathing, stamina, mental focus, and good alignment.

It is best to practice Pilates little and often at first rather than having long but occasional sessions. This will help you to build up your strength and understanding of the Pilates approach gradually. If possible, try to make time to practice Pilates every day, even if it is for only a few minutes.

INTRODUCTION
The following exercises are an introduction and are no substitute for a Pilates trainer-directed class. Take your time to read all the exercises before you begin to practice. Try each exercise a few times. Find your own comfort level by using mental focus to help yourself feel and respect your physical limits.

Always take your time. Even though these exercises may seem to be very gentle, they are based on the unique understanding of anatomy and physiology of Joseph Pilates and can have a powerful effect on your body.

THE EXERCISES
Aims: Each exercise has an introduction which gives you a brief overview of what the exercise is intended to do. These aims are not intended to be reached instantly but will come only with slow, diligent, and gentle practice. Remember that everybody is different, so you have to find a pace that suits you. The only way this is possible is by taking your time and being in tune with your body.

Placing a folded towel or pillow under your head helps to keep your neck in good alignment, but only if it is at the right height. Spend some time experimenting with different heights to see what feels most comfortable.

Don't try to do too many exercises at once when you begin practicing Pilates. Although some techniques appear to be very easy, they work on your body at a deep muscular level.

separate steps, but one fluid, relaxed movement that starts with your first deep breath and ends only when you return to the starting position.

Safety Points: It is essential that you read the safety points for each exercise before you start to practice the technique. This will ensure that you are aware of any conditions that may cause problems or any other essential safety factors. Naturally, all combinations of conditions and exercises that could cause problems cannot be foreseen. In general, you should check with a medical professional if you have any questions about your health or the suitability of these exercises for you. The need to see a medical professional, whether this happens to be an osteopath, physiotherapist, or physician, if you are in doubt cannot be overemphasized.

Equipment: You don't need any special equipment to practice the Pilates exercises in this book. However, supporting the back of your head with a small pillow when you are lying on the floor will help to keep the neck in alignment. In addition, you may find it comfortable to place a pillow or folded towel under any parts of your body that come into contact with a hard surface. Some exercises require a chair or a scarf.

Action: The exercises in this book are presented in a step-by-step manner so that you can see exactly what you are aiming for at each stage. However, remember that each exercise is not a series of

In general, the slow nature of Pilates techniques and the emphasis on controlled, natural movement will help you to protect your body. However, make sure that you read all the safety advice before you begin.

standing **Posture**

This step-by-step process describes how to create a good, stable standing posture by working slowly up your body, centering and relaxing each area in turn. This will give you the starting point for more efficient and relaxed movement in all the standing exercises. You may find it helpful to practice with a partner who can give you feedback on how your posture looks.

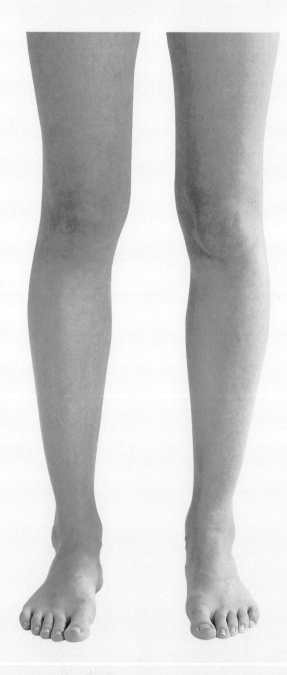

HOW TO BEGIN

Stand, with your feet about 4 inches apart, your arms hanging down by your sides, and your shoulders as relaxed as possible. It's helpful to stand in front of a mirror, particularly when you first start to practice Pilates, as this will give you a better idea of how you hold yourself. Slowly become aware of any tensions in your body, then gradually move your body in circles, then forward and backward, and finally to the left and to the right. Try to find the central, relaxed point, performing each movement gently, using the minimum of effort and covering the minimum distance. Then, bring your attention to each area of your body in turn, as described below and on the following pages, to release tension. Notice how each area feels when it is relaxed, then breathe deeply in and out five times before you move on.

FEET

Focus on your feet. Be aware of how your weight is distributed between the insides and outsides, and heels and balls of your feet. Gently sway your body, backward and forward, from side to side, and round in circles, to distribute your weight more evenly. You may notice tension in other areas of your body, but keep your attention on your feet. Don't spend more than a minute on this as your attention will fade.

You begin this exercise by focusing on the feet because they form the base for your entire body and your weight. It is essential to establish good grounding right at the start if your standing posture is to be centered and stable. From here, move up the rest of the body with patient attention.

CALF MUSCLES

Move your attention to your calf muscles and your shins. Again, shift your weight gently in all directions, noticing how the tension builds and relaxes. When you find the most central point, relax into it and breathe deeply in and out five times.

KNEES

Concentrate on your kneecaps. Do you feel tension or pressure in these areas? If so, shift your weight gently in all directions until you feel the knees release or unlock. Check that the soles of your feet and your calves remain relaxed throughout this stage. Hold this position and take five deep breaths in and out.

THIGH MUSCLES

Many people think that hard thigh muscles have the best kind of tone, but your thighs actually need to be relaxed as well as strong. It can be difficult to release tension from the thighs, so take as much time as you need when working on this area. Shift your weight in circles, backward and forward, and from side to side until you feel your thighs relax. Take five breaths and relax.

PELVIS AND BUTTOCKS

This is the center of your posture. To find a neutral, relaxed position, first gently and slowly tip your pelvis forward and backward (tucking your tailbone in and out) until you feel the place where there is the least amount of tension. Once you have done this, start shifting your weight from left to right until your pelvis is as central as possible and you feel near-equal pressure on your feet. This is the neutral pelvis position, which you want to adopt in all the exercises. Slowly scan up your lower body and check that you are maintaining the releasing feeling in your feet, calves, knees, and thighs. Hold this position and breathe in and out five times.

Getting your pelvis into a neutral and tension-free position is central to the Pilates approach and a key factor in almost all Pilates exercises. However, many people find that the pelvis and buttocks are one of the toughest areas of the body to relax. Take your time and be patient.

standing **Posture**

As you start to concentrate on the upper body, you may find that the lower areas move out of alignment. Keep checking the areas of the body you have centered and bring them back into good alignment as you continue working upward. The more often you do this exercise, the easier it will get. Try practicing it whenever you are waiting for someone or standing in a queue.

STOMACH WALL

Bring your attention to the abdomen. Tighten your stomach muscles as much as possible, then release. Try to find a middle tension between full tightening and total relaxation as this will help you to develop good abdominal muscle tone. In addition, shift your weight gently forward and backward, left and right, and in circles until you feel your abdominals reach the middle point of tension. Hold and breathe five times.

BACK

Your lower back is the most vulnerable part of your back. To release tension here, concentrate on relaxing the area between your buttocks and shoulder blades. First, tuck your tailbone in slowly and at the same

Keeping good muscle tone in the abdominal area will help you to protect your lower back. Good muscle tone here gives your body the core stability it needs in order to keep a good posture during movement.

Millions of people suffer from lower back pain and about 80 percent of these problems are muscular. A regular practice of Pilates will help you to retrain your back muscles into a state of optimum relaxation, helping you to move more efficiently and reduce any risk of injury.

time raise your shoulders gently upward. You will feel the tension run along the entire length of your spine. Once you are aware of tension building up, stop and return to your original position.

Now, perform the opposite action. Bring your shoulder blades backward and downward while at the same time raising your tailbone. Again, as soon as you feel tension building, stop and gently return to your starting position. Move gently and slowly between these two actions until you find the point that holds the least tension. Hold this position and breathe deeply in and out five times.

CHEST

Poor tone in the chest can cause poor posture, which will restrict your breathing. Finding the middle area between deep breathing and shallow breathing and relaxing into it is the objective here. Take some shallow, then some deep breaths, breathing into your back and the sides of your ribcage. Allow your breath to find a middle depth and breathe in and out five times. Take your attention to the feet and work your way up your body, checking you are retaining a relaxed posture. Take five breaths and relax.

SHOULDERS

Gently pull your shoulders backward and upward as tightly as you are able to without straining. Then, bring your shoulders down and forward. Again, find the middle ground, relax into it, and take five breaths in and out. Take another five breaths and relax.

ARMS

Let your arms hang as dead weights and then gently turn them inward and outward. In addition, slowly swing your arms backward and forward to find that all-important tension-free central point. Take five breaths and relax into your posture.

NECK

To find a tension-free position for the neck, use forward-bending, backward-bending, looking-right and looking-left movements. You can also tip your head sideways to the left and right. Take your time to work between the movements and find a middle point of tension release. Take five breaths, then take your attention to your feet, and work your way up the body to ensure your posture is relaxed throughout.

SUMMARY

This is a simple approach to finding Pilates control in a standing position, which you can practice at any time. The tension-release procedures take time and practice to master. However, you should experience a feeling of lightness, as though your body is lifting upward rather than sinking downward.

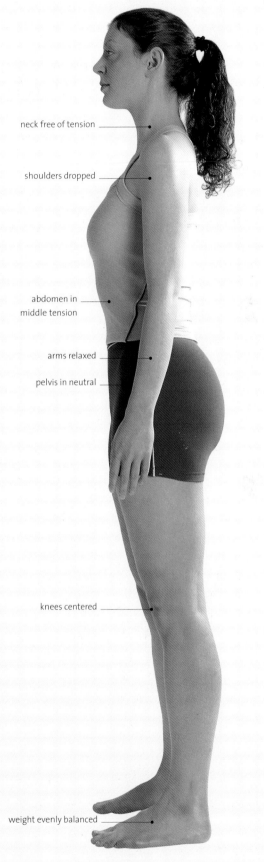

neck free of tension

shoulders dropped

abdomen in middle tension

arms relaxed

pelvis in neutral

knees centered

weight evenly balanced

single light **Arms**

Aim: To be able to keep the shoulders down and relaxed while moving your arms. This exercise encourages you to use the major and minor shoulder muscles in a more efficient manner and draw the shoulder blades down the back. There are four basic actions, which enable you to practice the movements of your arms in different directions.

ACTION NO.1

left hand rests
on right shoulder

right hand
rests on thigh

1 Stand in a relaxed Standing Position with your feet hip-width apart. Place your left hand on your right shoulder. Gently pull your lower abdominal muscles toward your spine and pull up on your pelvic floor muscles. Breathe into the sides of your ribcage and your back to prepare for movement.

2 Breathing out, raise your right arm out to your side, turning your palm upward. Use your left hand to check that you are keeping your right shoulder down and keep your neck and shoulder-blade area free of tension. Raise your upper arm to shoulder level, then breathe in, and lower your arm.

ACTION NO. 2

1 This is similar to Action No. 1 but you bring your right arm forward rather than to the side as you breathe out. Your palm should face you, thumb side up, as you raise your arm. When the arm reaches shoulder level, breathe in, and let your arm gently float back down to your side. Change sides and repeat with your left arm. This is one set. Perform 7–10 sets.

3 Bring the palm of your right hand down to touch the outside of your thigh, keeping your right shoulder relaxed. Place your right hand on your left shoulder and raise your left arm in the same way. This is one set. Repeat 7–10 sets.

SAFETY POINTS

• Don't try this exercise if you have any doubts about the stability of your shoulders. If you have ever dislocated your shoulder or are concerned about arthritis, seek medical advice.

• Do not use this exercise as rehabilitation after injury or while you are in pain.

double light **Arms**

Aim: To raise both arms out and to the sides. This exercise is a development of Single Light Arms and encourages you to use your upper body without tensing your shoulder muscles. Make sure that you have mastered the previous exercise before trying this—your shoulder muscles should not rise upward when you raise up your arms.

ACTION NO.1

palms facing inward

shoulder relaxed

hips level

1 Stand in a relaxed Standing Position and engage your abdominal muscles and pelvic floor. Drop your shoulders and take a deep breath into the back and sides of the ribcage to prepare for relaxed movement. Breathe out and slowly raise your arms out to the sides, turning your palms to face upward.

SAFETY POINTS

• Don't try this exercise if you are worried about the stability of your shoulders. If you have suffered a shoulder dislocation at any time or are concerned about arthritis, seek medical advice.

• Do not use this exercise as a rehabilitation technique after injury or if you are in pain.

feet parallel to each other

ACTION NO. 2

1 Drop your shoulders, and breathe deeply into your back and the sides of your ribcage. Breathe out and slowly raise your arms in front of you to shoulder level, turning your palms to face inward. Breathing in, let your arms drop back down to your sides. Keep your shoulders down throughout the exercise. Repeat 7–10 times.

2 Continue raising your arms above your head until your palms are facing each other and your fingers are pointing upward. Keep your shoulders relaxed. As you breathe in, let your arms slowly drift down and place your palms on the outsides of your thighs. Repeat 7–10 times.

light arms & strong **Legs**

Aim: To improve your coordination and build up general relaxation and strength. This exercise combines gentle knee bends with Double Light Arms (Action No. 2). It gives you practice in moving effectively and coordinating different actions while retaining a stable posture.

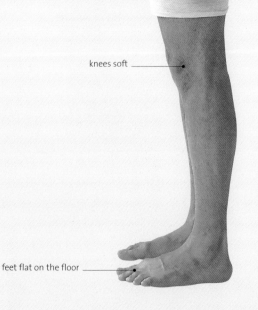

chest relaxed

good abdominal control

knees soft

feet flat on the floor

1 Begin in a relaxed Standing Position with your feet shoulder-width apart. Gently draw in your lower abdominal muscles to bring your navel toward your spine and raise your pelvic floor upward to ensure good stabilization. Breathe deeply into the sides of your ribcage and your back to prepare the body for relaxed movement.

SAFETY POINTS

• Do not try this exercise if you have weak or unstable shoulders or have suffered a recent injury.

• If you have pain or weakness in your knees, seek the advice of a medical professional before performing this exercise.

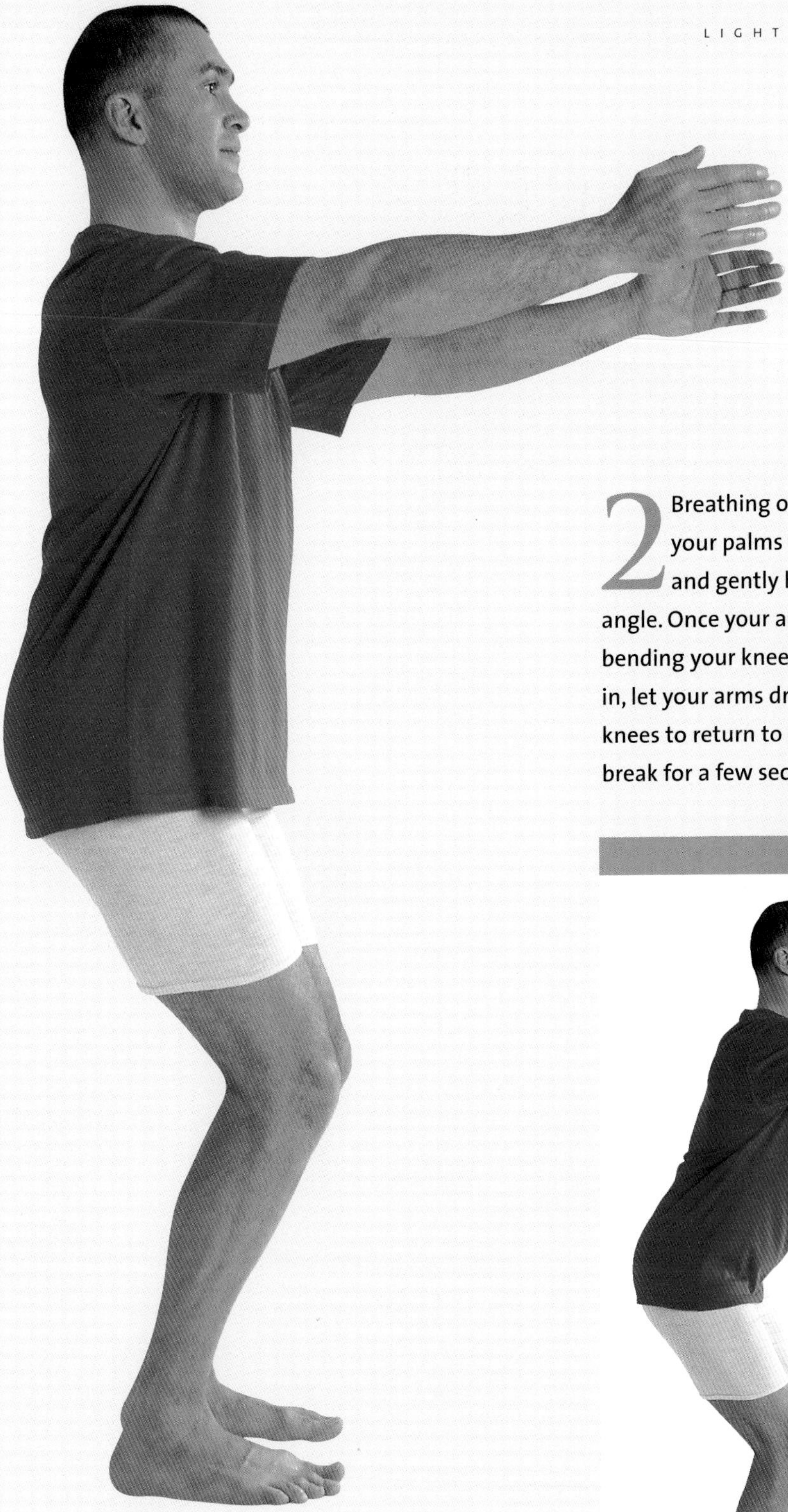

2 Breathing out, raise your arms in front, turning your palms to face slightly toward your body, and gently bend your knees to a 45-degree angle. Once your arms reach shoulder-level, stop bending your knees and raising your arms. Breathing in, let your arms drift downward, and straighten your knees to return to resume Standing Position. Take a break for a few seconds. Repeat 7–10 times

WATCH OUT

Make sure that you don't lean forward and lose your neutral pelvis position, as shown here. The shoulders are also tense and the chin is up, which has pushed the neck out of alignment.

upper body **Raises**

Aim: To practice an additional technique for good control of upper body movements. This exercise provides a gentle stretch for the chest muscles (pectorals), underarm muscles (latissimus dorsi), and shoulder muscles (deltoids) while keeping stability.

EQUIPMENT: A pole, scarf, or rope.

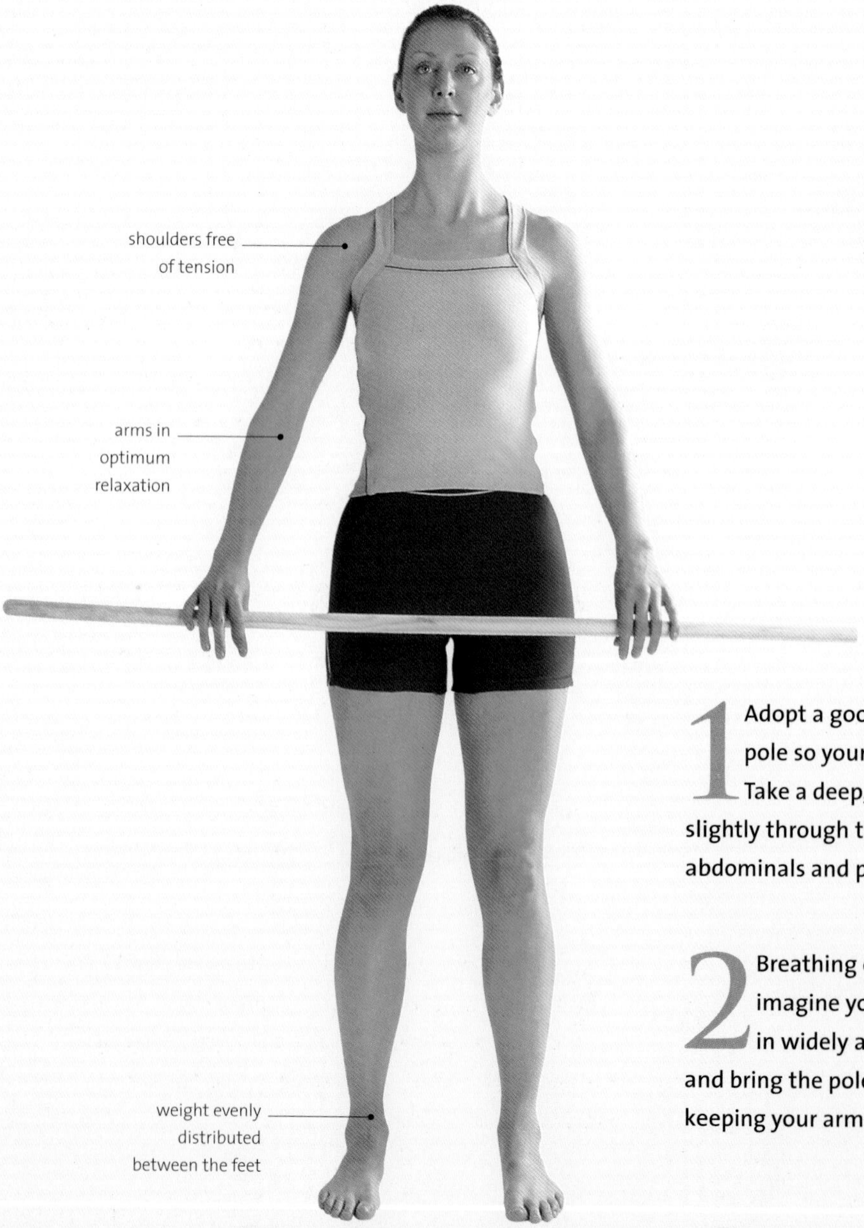

shoulders free of tension

arms in optimum relaxation

weight evenly distributed between the feet

1 Adopt a good Standing Position and hold your pole so your hands are shoulder-width apart. Take a deep, wide breath in and elevate up slightly through the spine. Gently pull in your lower abdominals and pull up on your pelvic floor.

2 Breathing out, drop your shoulders, and imagine your body sinking downward. Breathe in widely and deeply to prepare. Breathe out and bring the pole to the level of your forehead, keeping your arms extended and shoulders relaxed.

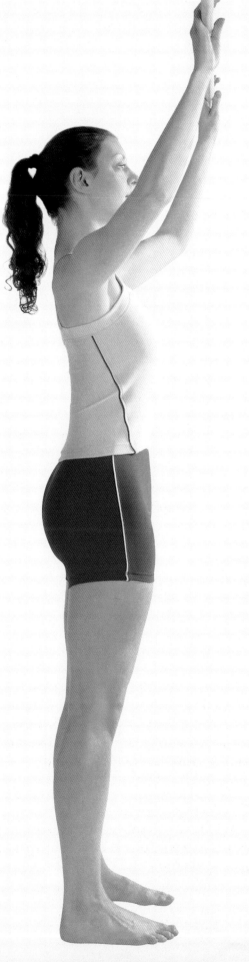

Keep a good standing posture as you raise your pole. Here, the back is overarched and the shoulders have been drawn upward, creating tension and misalignment.

SAFETY POINTS

• As with all upper-body exercises, you should not practice this technique if you have injured your shoulders or they are unstable.

• Don't do this exercise if you have a neck problem as this may be aggravated by raising up your arms.

3 Breathe in and let your arms rise upward until they are extended as high as you can comfortably reach. Breathe out and gently and slowly move your arms downward to your starting position. Repeat 7–10 times.

head in good alignment
with neck and shoulders

sitting **Posture**

Aim: To encourage you to sit in a good relaxed posture. Most people spend a lot of time sitting, but tend to slouch rather than sit upright. This exercise helps to retrain the body and you can practice it any time you are sitting down.

EQUIPMENT: One straight-backed chair.

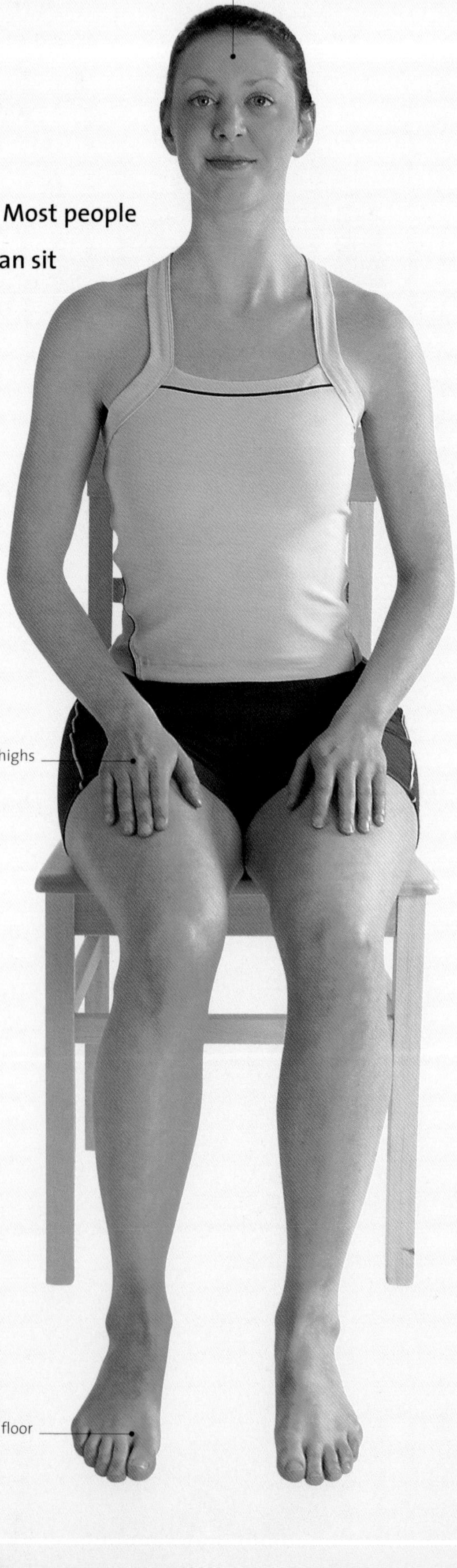

hands rest lightly on thighs

1 Sit on the front two-thirds of the chair with your feet placed flat on the floor and hip-width apart. (You can sit with your buttocks against the back of the chair if you are practicing this in your daily life but moving forward reduces the temptation to lean back.) Drop your shoulders, place your hands on your thighs and relax your pelvic floor muscles. Breathe in deeply and widely, projecting your breath into your back and the sides of your ribcage. Elevate up slightly through your spine to help straighten your posture.

SAFETY POINTS

• Do not hold this position for too long the first few times that you try it. It may take time for you to feel comfortable in a good sitting posture.

feet flat on floor

2 Breathe out with control, tightening the muscles of your pelvic floor to about 50 percent of your tension potential. Breathe in and release the tension in your pelvic floor, then breathe out, and tighten your pelvic floor just short of full tension. Breathe in again and release the tension, then breathe out, this time tightening your pelvic floor muscles to near-capacity tension. Breathe in and then out, then relax. Rest for 30–60 seconds. Repeat 3 times.

WATCH OUT

You want your spine to be erect without forcing it; it is arching too much here.

waist **Turns**

Aim: To increase the rotation of the lumbar spine. The lumbar spine joints run up the spine and rotate left to right and vice versa. Waist turns will increase the twisting ability of the lumbar spine, which will increase flexibility and reduce the risk of acute lower back pain.

EQUIPMENT: One straight-backed chair.

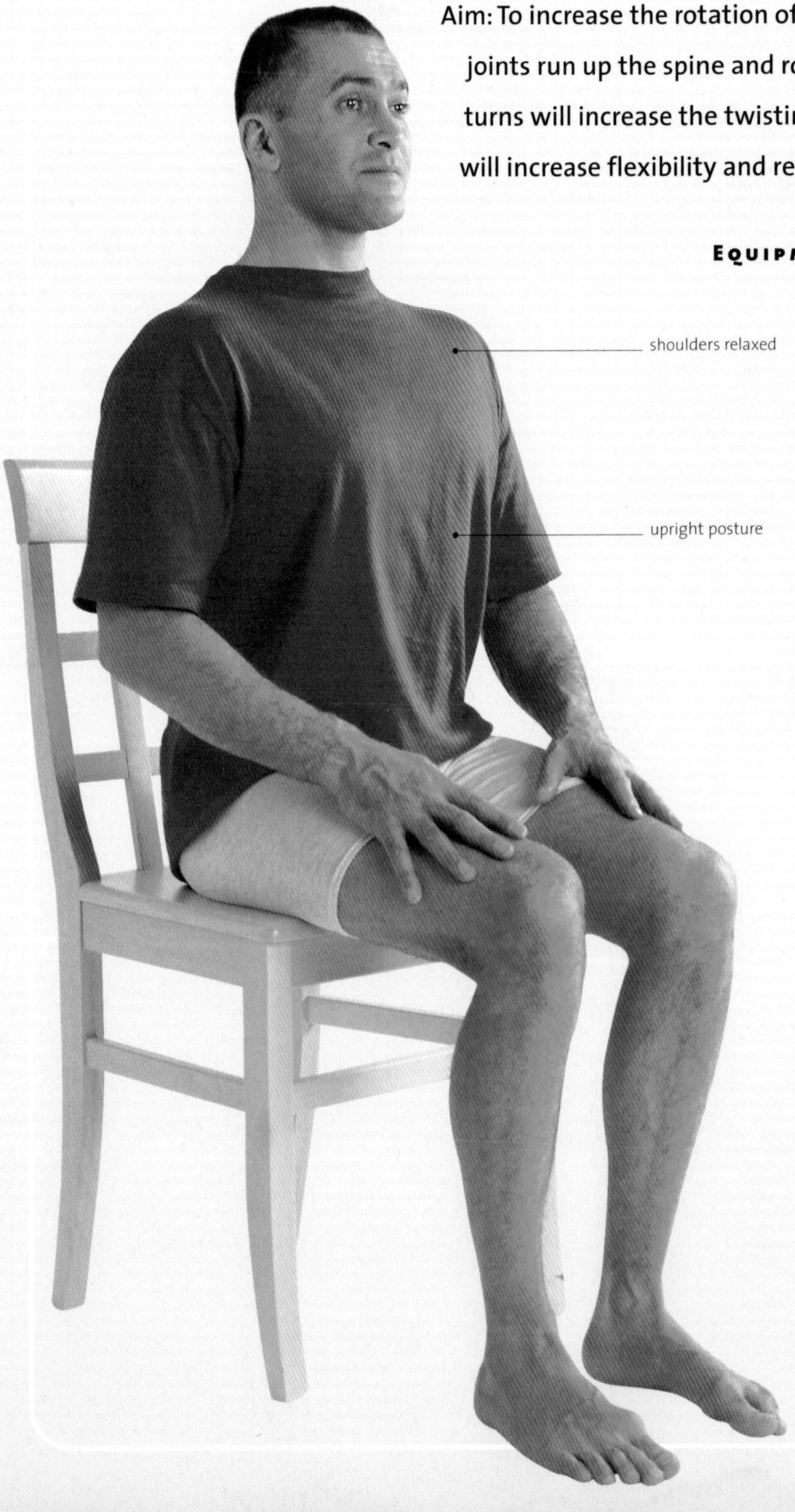

shoulders relaxed

upright posture

1 Sit on the front two-thirds of the chair, with your feet flat on the floor and hip-width apart. Place one hand on each thigh. Breathe in widely and deeply and extend your spine gently upward. Gently bring your abdominal muscles toward your spine and raise your pelvic floor muscles.

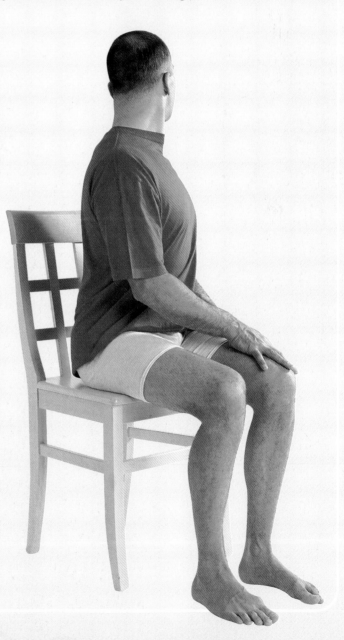

2 Breathe in and gently turn to look over your right shoulder, letting your head begin a turn that coils down the length of your spine. As your spine twists, place your left hand on your right thigh next to your right hand. Breathing in, uncoil by first turning back your head and allow the rest of your body to follow. Look back to the front and place your left hand back on your left thigh.

3 Repeat the same on the other side. Breathing in, turn to look over your left shoulder, and moving the right hand to rest on the left thigh. Again, let your head turning begin the movement round and back again as you breathe out. This completes one set. Repeat 7–10 times.

SAFETY POINTS

• It is important that your lower back and lumbar spine are injury-free before you do this exercise. Do not use this routine to heal lower back pain.

• If you feel or hear clicking or popping in the spine and it is not painful, then it is decompression of the joints and should be of no consequence.

• If you feel or hear clicking or popping and it continues as the exercise progresses, even if it is painless, then see a medical professional.

lateral **Lunges**

Aim: To stretch the sides of the ribcage and encourage movement of the lower back and lumbar spine. This exercise also works the waist muscles, giving you more mobility, and helps you to practice keeping the shoulder muscles stable.

EQUIPMENT: One straight-backed chair.

arms relaxed

body centered

1 Sit astride a chair backward with your feet flat on the floor and comfortably apart. Place both of your hands on the back of the chair and breathe deeply into your back and the sides of your ribcage to prepare the body for movement.

feet flat on floor

2 Gently bring your abdominal muscles toward your spine and raise your pelvic floor muscles. Breathing out, raise your right arm over your head, turning your palm so that it faces toward your left side. Breathe in deeply and widely.

shoulder stays relaxed as arm raises up

3 Breathing out, lean your upper body slowly to your left. Breathe in, straighten up, and let your arm drift slowly down until you can place your right hand back on the chair. Repeat on the other side to make one set. Repeat 7–10 times.

SAFETY POINTS

• Do not do this exercise if either of your shoulders is unstable, if you have any lower back problems, or have recently sustained an injury.

• If you are in any doubt about the suitability of this exercise, please seek medical advice.

lateral **Breathing**

Aim: To practice effective lateral breathing. Lateral breathing is the most effective form of breathing to use when you are exercising and helps you to create greater postural stability. Using a scarf helps you to focus your attention on directing your breathing into your back and the sides of your ribcage rather than the upper chest area.

EQUIPMENT: A long scarf or dishtowel.

hands hold scarf gently but firmly

1 Kneel with your knees as closely together as is comfortable and your buttocks resting on your heels. Pull the scarf around the bottom third of your chest and ribcage. Holding the ends firmly but gently in your hands, drop your shoulders and move your elbows a few inches away from the side of your body. Cross your hands over your chest to help you pull the ends of the scarf in a smooth movement.

SAFETY POINTS

• Older people should perform this exercise while sitting down rather than standing up.

• Breathe in and out slowly and smoothly. If you start to feel dizzy at any point during the exercise—stop and breathe normally.

If you find it uncomfortable to kneel, try standing or sitting on a chair instead. You can practice the technique just as well in these positions.

2 Keeping a firm, gentle hold, take a deep breath into your back and the sides of your ribcage, feeling the gentle resistance as you push into the scarf. Slacken your hold slightly so that the scarf expands as you breathe in but still maintains some resistance. As you breathe out, pull the scarf a little tighter. This helps you to expel as much air as possible from the lungs. Repeat slowly and gently 7-10 times.

finding pelvic **Neutral**

Aim: To find the most relaxed and neutral resting position for your hips and back. Working through these exercises will help you find a point of relaxation deep in your hips and pelvis, which helps to bring your body into natural alignment and place the least amount of pressure on your joints. Once you've found pelvic neutral, incorporate it into all the exercises.

EQUIPMENT: Folded towel or small pillow to place under the back of the head.

1 Lie on your back and place your head on a pillow to keep your neck relaxed and straight. Bend your knees, with your feet parallel to each other, a few inches apart, and flat on the floor. Flatten your lower back as far toward the floor as you can comfortably go and gently pull in your abdominal muscles. Feel the tension build, then release it.

knees bent so that feet lie flat on the ground

abdominal muscles in
optimum tension

2 Perform the opposite action by gently arching
your back upward, again as far as you can
comfortably go. Feel this tension build, then
release it. Now try to find the relaxed, central point
between these two extreme positions.

SAFETY POINTS

• If you feel any pain when you are stretching your
lower back and tightening your abdominal
muscles, stop the exercise immediately. Seek advice
from a medical professional before continuing.

3 Tighten your right hip by raising it closer to the
bottom right ribs. Relax it gently. Then, tighten
your left hip by raising it closer to the bottom
left ribs. Relax it gently. Try to find the relaxed, central
point between the right and left sides of your pelvis.
Tighten your left hip by raising it closer to the bottom
left ribs. Relax it gently. Try to find the relaxed, central
point between the right and left sides of your pelvis.

4 Work with these actions until you find a
relaxed pelvis position—you are looking for a
neutral area between all four movements. This
pelvic position will enable you to perform the other
exercises in this book with more comfort and ease. It
will also help you to work on and improve your overall
posture and learn the importance of the central area
of the body to stability, flexibility, and strength.

focus your attention
on this central area

relaxation **Position**

Aim: To bring the mind and body together in a relaxed mode in preparation for exercise. Each of the floor exercises begins with the relaxation position to help you bring your muscles into a state of optimum relaxation rather than one of semitension, which creates inefficient movement. You also finish the exercises in this position.

EQUIPMENT: Folded towel or small pillow to place under the back of the head.

1 Lie on your back, resting your head on a pillow or folded towel to keep the neck straight and relaxed. Bend your knees and slide the feet up toward your hips until they reach a comfortable position. Keep the feet parallel and a few inches apart. Place your hands on your abdomen and imagine your body lengthening and widening. Be aware of the floor under your body, allowing yourself to sink into it. Focus on your feet, feeling them relax into the floor, then work up the body, relaxing your calves and thighs, pelvis, back, neck, and back of the head.

SAFETY POINTS

• Do not stay in the Relaxation Position for more than 5 minutes when you first try it as you may find it difficult to get up from the floor afterward.

• Try 5 minutes every day in the first week, progressing to 10 minutes in the second week.

• To get up from this position, roll onto your side, then move onto all fours, and kneel to stand up.

hands rest lightly
on the abdomen

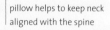

pillow helps to keep neck
aligned with the spine

relaxation position and **Breathing**

Aim: To combine lateral or thoracic breathing with the relaxation position. This exercise allows you to practice the breathing while you are lying down. Placing your hands on your lower ribcage helps you to direct your breath correctly. Once you have grown accustomed to lateral breathing, this is an exercise that you can practice for prolonged periods of time.

1 Lie in the Relaxation Position with a pillow or folded towel under your head. Make sure that your neck feels free and comfortable and is properly aligned with your spine—you may need to experiment with different thicknesses of towel to achieve a position that is right for you. Move your hands to rest gently on the lower third of your ribcage. Breathe deeply and gently into your back and the sides of your lower ribs, feeling them expand under your hands and gently move downward into the floor. Then, gently breathe out with good control, feeling the ribs contract under your hands and relaxing them downward. Repeat this 7–10 times, maintaining a good pelvic neutral position.

SAFETY POINTS

• If you notice your back starting to stiffen or ache while you are in Relaxation Position, gently bring your knees toward your chest and roll onto your side to get out of the position safely.

• Don't breathe too quickly or too deeply when you begin practicing this exercise.

• If you start to feel dizzy when practicing the breathing, breathe normally but remain in the Relaxation Position for at least a minute before rolling over to your side to get up.

relaxation position, breathing
and Stabilizing

Aim: To begin to combine the Relaxation Position, your breathing, and stabilization to develop a good foundation for all future exercises and general posture. Learning to keep your central torso under control while you breathe helps you to improve your core stability, which is one of the key factors involved in the Pilates approach to exercise.

EQUIPMENT: Folded towel or small pillow to place under the back of the head.

1 Begin in the Relaxation Position, again ensuring that your neck is in a comfortable position. Place both of your hands on the front of your hips, with your fingertips together, pointing slightly downward and resting near or on your pubic bone. Make sure your pelvis and hips are resting comfortably in the neutral position (perform the pelvic neutral exercises on pages 54–55 if necessary).

(perform the pelvic neutral exercises on pages 54–55 if necessary).

SAFETY POINTS

• Make all your initial movements very small. This will help to prevent you from straining.

• You may feel or hear clicking or cracking in your lower or middle back. This is common and you do not need to stop the exercise unless you feel pain.

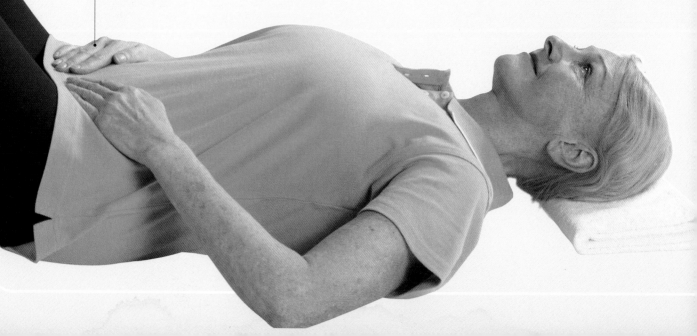

hands rest on the pelvic region

RELAXATION POSITION, BREATHING AND STABILIZING **59**

2 Take a few controlled, deep breaths, retaining a good, relaxed posture. Then, slide your hands up to your lower ribcage without breaking your body contact. Breathe deeply into the sides of your lower ribs and into the ground, feeling your ribcage expanding outward and downward.

3 As you breathe out, engage the muscles of the pelvic floor by raising them upward and gently pull in your lower abdominal muscles. Keep the pelvis in neutral, breathe in, and relax. Repeat 7–10 times. When you have mastered this technique, try breathing in and out while holding your pelvis in the neutral position, maintaining your pelvic floor tone, and pulling in your lower abdominal muscles.

hands rest on the lower ribcage

the **Backstroke**

Aim: To encourage the further development of coordinated movement. Joseph Pilates would have used this technique to help in the rehabilitation of neurologically injured patients. However, it also benefits the healthy person as the alternate hand-foot coordination promotes more efficient coordinated movement.

EQUIPMENT: Folded towel or small pillow to place under the back of the head.

1 Begin in the Relaxation Position. Bring your pelvis into neutral, gently pull your abdominal muscles toward your spine, and raise your pelvic floor muscles. Breathing out, slide your left leg until it is flat on the floor and raise your right arm up above the head in a fluid backstroke swimming action until it is lying on the floor behind you, or at least as close to the floor as it will comfortably go.

arm slightly bent at the elbow to keep it relaxed

2 Breathing in, gently return your left leg and right arm to the starting Relaxation Position in one smooth movement. When you first start this exercise, don't make the movements too fast or sudden—this can cause straining of the muscles.

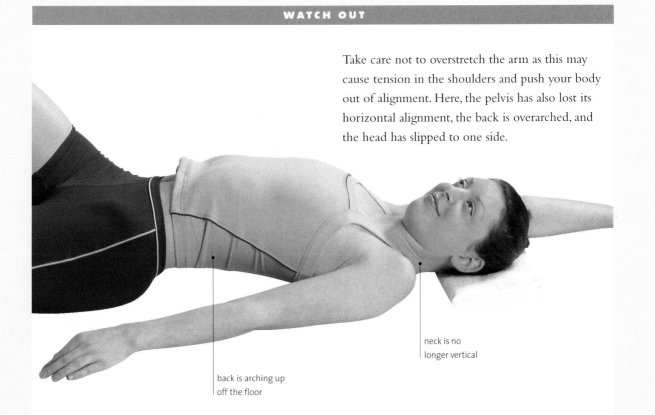

3 Breathe out and repeat on your other side, sliding your right leg down until it is lying flat on the floor and raising the left arm above your head, again until it is lying on the floor or as close to the floor as you can comfortably get it. Keep the arm slightly bent so that it stays relaxed and don't strain to push it down to the floor. This completes one set. Repeat the exercise 7–10 times.

SAFETY POINTS

• Your lower back may want to arch upward when you do this but keep the pelvic neutral position.

• As you move the arm back, you increase the tension on your abdominal muscles. Begin and finish the movement slowly to prevent straining.

WATCH OUT

Take care not to overstretch the arm as this may cause tension in the shoulders and push your body out of alignment. Here, the pelvis has also lost its horizontal alignment, the back is overarched, and the head has slipped to one side.

neck is no longer vertical

back is arching up off the floor

upper body **Control**

Aim: To develop good control of your arms while maintaining stabilization and alignment. In this exercise, you are learning how to move your arms while keeping your shoulder blades drawn downwards. Over time, this will help you to develop good upper body control, which will help you in other exercises and in your everyday activities.

EQUIPMENT: Folded towel or small pillow to place under the back of the head.

1 Begin in the Relaxation Position with your arms by your sides. Bring your pelvis into neutral and take a deep, wide breath in to prepare. Breathe out and gently tighten your abdominals and pelvic floor muscles. Continuing to breathe out, slide your right arm up above your head, turning your palm to face upwards and drawing your shoulder blade slightly downwards. Keep your elbow slightly bent so that your arm and shoulder stay relaxed.

pelvis in neutral

lower body remains still but relaxed

arm kept in state of optimum relaxation

2 There may be an automatic tendency for your back to arch upward while you are in the process of raising your arm above your head. Be aware of this and raise your arm only as high as it will comfortably go, keeping your pelvis in the neutral position. As you breathe in, slide your right arm back along the floor to rest by your side again.

SAFETY POINTS

• Pain and clicking in the shoulders and lower back that are not repeated or accompanied by pain usually denote pressure releasing from the joints. However, stop the exercise immediately and seek the advice of a medical professional if you also feel pain or the noise is recurrent.

3 Breathing out, slide your left arm up above your head in the same way, again taking care not to overarch the back or allow the shoulder to move off the floor. Then, bring the left arm back to your side as you breathe in deeply and widely. This completes one set. Repeat 7–10 times.

neck **Rolls**

Aim: To release the tension in the rotation muscles of the neck. This exercise allows you to practise good neck movement while maintaining correct alignment of your head, neck and spine. It also encourages you to keep your shoulders stable and the shoulder blades drawn downwards into the back, which is an important aspect of stabilization.

EQUIPMENT: Folded towel or small pillow to place under the back of the head.

1 Begin this exercise in the Relaxation Position with your hands by your sides or on your abdomen, whichever you find most comfortable. Check that your spine alignment is correct before you begin. Also make sure that your head and neck are straight and relaxed. Focus your attention on your pelvis and check that it is in the neutral position. Take a controlled deep breath into your back and the sides of your lower ribs to prepare for relaxed movement.

SAFETY POINTS

• You may hear your neck cracking, clicking, or popping as you perform these exercises. In general, these noises are quite innocent, but if you feel any pain at the same time, stop immediately.

• If you feel any pins and needles or tingling in your hands or feet, stop the exercise.

head correctly aligned with the spine

muscles held in optimum relaxation

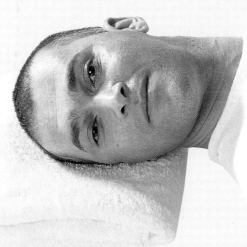

2 As you breathe out, turn your head to the right, keeping your body as relaxed as possible and maintaining your spine alignment.

3 Breathe in and return your head to the face-up position, then slowly breathe out again, and turn it to the left. Breathe in and bring your head back to the starting position. This completes one set. Repeat it 7–10 times.

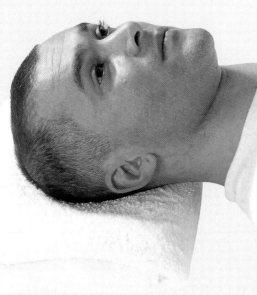

chin tucks—**Neck stretch**

Aim: To stretch and release the muscles and joints of the neck. Like the previous exercise, this technique helps you to train your body to make effective neck movements while retaining stabilization and good alignment of the spine, head, and neck. It also provides good practice in keeping the shoulders relaxed as you move the head and neck.

EQUIPMENT: Folded towel or small pillow to place under the back of the head.

1 Lie in the Relaxation Position with your hands resting on your abdomen or by the sides of your body. Breathe gently into your back and the sides of the lower ribs and slowly tuck your chin into your throat, making sure that you keep the back of your head on the pillow. You should feel the back of your neck gently stretch as you practice this. When you feel the tension has built to a comfortable level, stop the movement and relax into the posture.

SAFETY POINTS

• You should not experience any pain in your neck.

• If you feel or hear cracking, clicking, or popping, return to the starting position. Repeat the movement but stop before the sound or feeling is felt. In the majority of cases, this is harmless. However, if you feel pain, seek medical advice.

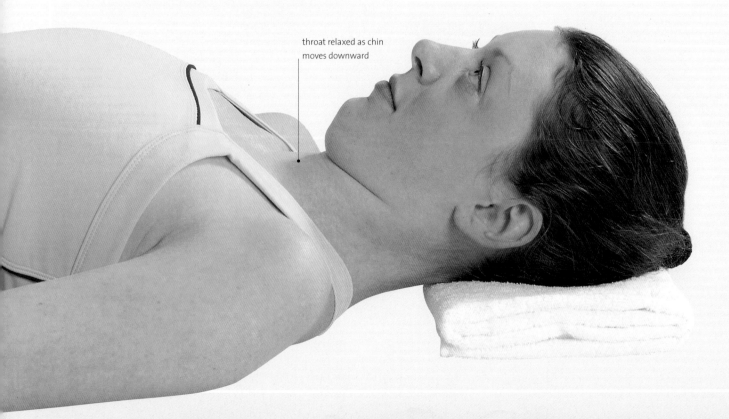

throat relaxed as chin moves downward

2 As you slowly breathe out with control, return
your head to the neutral starting position. Rest
here for about 30 seconds. This rest period gives
you the chance to check that your breathing is relaxed
and your alignment remains good. Resting also
prevents you from turning the technique into a
continuous, pulsing movement, which could build up
tension in the neck. Repeat this stretch 7–10 times,
incorporating the rest period each time.

WATCH OUT

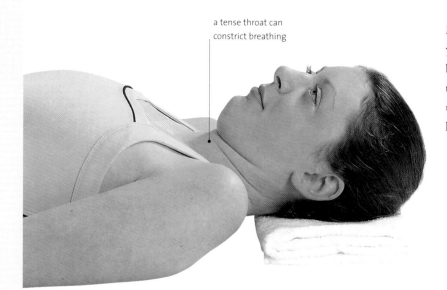

a tense throat can
constrict breathing

Make sure that you keep
your shoulders relaxed as you
bring the chin down. Here,
the shoulders have moved
upward so the neck is not
lengthening properly.

chest and arm **Opening**

Aim: To provide a good stretching motion for the chest muscles, the upper ribs, and the collarbone. In addition, this exercise will also help to turn the upper spine and stretch the neck muscles. It helps you to practice smooth movement and coordinating your breath with your actions. Remember that forcing your spine beyond comfort level can be dangerous.

EQUIPMENT: Two small pillows or towels, to place under the head and between the knees.

1 Begin in the Relaxation Position with a pillow or towel under your head. Place a second pillow or folded towel between your knees and relax for 30 seconds. Move your arms out to the sides, at right angles to your body and take a deep, wide breath in.

SAFETY POINTS

• Be aware that your spine, from your lower back to the base of your neck, is twisting in this exercise. Stop if you feel discomfort at any point.

• This exercise should not be performed if you have been told by a medical professional that you have a weak disk, joint irritation, any ligament instability, or any signs of inflammation.

arm slightly bent
to keep it relaxed

head turns, maintaining
good spine alignment

knees move to
the side

2 Breathing out, gently tighten your abdominal
muscles while drawing up your pelvic floor.
Turn your body to the left, bringing your right
hand to rest on your left hand, letting your knees
gently fall to the ground, and turning your head at the
same time. You should now be lying on your side with
your knees bent and your arms stretched out in front
of you at shoulder height. Breathe in and relax.

feet together

3 Breathe in and slowly move your right arm to
the floor behind you, keeping your arm at
shoulder level. Breathe out and bring your right
arm back to the left. Repeat 7–10 times. Return to the
Relaxation Position and repeat on the other side.

arm remains in
relaxed position

shoulder **Stretch**

Aim: To improve stability and control and to release tension from the upper body. This exercise helps you to become aware of movement in the upper back and around the shoulder blades, which play an important part in providing stabilization. It also enables you to practice good arm movement while keeping your shoulders relaxed.

EQUIPMENT: Folded towel or small pillow to place under the back of the head.

1 Begin in the Relaxation Position. Raise both of your arms, with your palms facing each other and your elbows slightly bent. Bring your pelvis into neutral and keep it stable by bringing your abdominal muscles toward your spine and raising the pelvic floor. Breathe deeply into your back and your lower ribs to prepare for relaxed movement.

palms facing each other

2 Breathe out and stretch your arms upward, relaxing your shoulders as much as possible and keeping your arms slightly bent. Your shoulder blades will slide outward as you stretch, which will help to reduce the pressure in your shoulders. Breathe in and return to your starting position. Repeat the stretch 7–10 times.

• If you have had any shoulder problems, especially dislocations or increasing instability, seek medical advice before performing this exercise. Again, if you hear or feel clicks or pops that are recurrent or painful, see a medical professional.

WATCH OUT

Make sure that you keep neutral pelvis as you stretch up, or you may overarch your back. Here, the arms and hands are also tense, so the shoulders have tightened, pulling the body out of alignment.

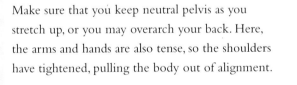

cross-over **Stretch**

Aim: To increase the release of the Shoulder Stretch. Like the previous exercise, this technique encourages you to move the arms without tensing up your shoulders and contracting the muscles around your shoulder blades. With time and practice, this exercise will help you to increase the mobility of your shoulders and upper back.

EQUIPMENT: Folded towel or small pillow to place under the back of the head.

1 Lie in the Relaxation Position and raise your arms with your palms facing each other. Keep your shoulders relaxed. Stabilize your pelvis into neutral and breathe deeply into the back and lower ribs to prepare for the stretch.

SAFETY POINTS

• If you have had any shoulder problems, in particular dislocation or increasing instability, it is best to seek advice from a medical professional before performing this exercise.

head turns gently
to the right

2 Breathe out and tighten your abdominals and pelvic floor muscles. Continuing to breathe out, move your left arm to cross your right arm (keep your right arm still). At the same time, turn your head and look to your left. Breathe in and hold this position. Breathe out and return your head to the face-up position and uncross your arms so that the palms are facing each other again. Repeat 7–10 times.

3 Do the same on your other side, this time moving your right arm to cross your left and turning your head to look to your right. Again, repeat the technique 7–10 times. After the final repetition, let your arms drift slowly back down to the ground as you breathe out.

arms drop slowly
downward

back **Curls**

Aim: To improve the movement of the individual vertebrae and release tension in the spinal muscles. When the individual spinal joints are stiff, the last vertebral joint bears much of the burden of movement. This can cause overstretching of the ligaments and may lead to back pain.

hands held loosely
by the sides

knees soft rather
than locked

1 Stand in a relaxed Standing Position with your back against a stable wall and your feet far enough away so that your legs are parallel with the wall. Place your feet so that they are hip-width apart, pointing forward and parallel to each other, and keep your knees relaxed. Try to bring your shoulders back against the wall—do not strain if you cannot touch the wall easily but bring the shoulders as close to it as you can.

SAFETY POINTS

• Do not perform this bending movement jerkily, but curl and uncurl slowly and smoothly.

• You may feel dizzy when you perform this exercise for the first time. If your dizziness does not subside soon after you have returned upright— seek medical advice and have your blood pressure checked. It may be high or too low.

• Any pins and needles or tingling in your face, arms, or feet is a sign to seek medical advice.

• If you feel or hear a clicking or popping noise as you bend down or up, this is probably just pressure releasing from the joints. However, if the clicking or popping hurts, seek medical advice.

2 Breathe into your back and lower ribs. Breathe out and engage your lower abdominals and pelvic floor muscles. At the same time, begin to roll your chin down toward your throat. Let your arms hang down as you bend forward. Continue to breathe out and curl down, vertebra by vertebra, as your hands drop toward the floor.

back curling softly downward

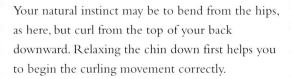

WATCH OUT

Your natural instinct may be to bend from the hips, as here, but curl from the top of your back downward. Relaxing the chin down first helps you to begin the curling movement correctly.

3 Reach down to a level that you are both comfortable with and can control. When you have reached this point, begin to breathe in and uncurl slowly and carefully, maintaining the abdominal and pelvic floor tone. Once you have reached the upright position, take a few seconds to get your orientation back. Repeat 7–10 times.

lower back **Turns**

Aim: To improve rotation of the lumbar spine and tone the waist muscles. This exercise gives you good practice of twisting the spine while retaining your core stability and helps you to develop control of the pelvic neutral position. Over time, it will increase the mobility of your back, which will benefit your daily activities as well as other exercises.

EQUIPMENT: Folded towel or small pillow.

abdominals drawn in to help stabilize the pelvis in neutral

1 Lie in the Relaxation Position and stretch out your arms until they are at 90 degrees from the body with your palms facing upward. Bring your pelvis into neutral and engage your abdominal and pelvic floor muscles. Breathe in deeply and widely.

SAFETY POINTS

• Particular care must be taken with this exercise—very slow movement is essential.

• Do not overstrain. If your knees move only a few inches, this is enough to work the body.

• Minor back strains and disk irritations will be exacerbated with this exercise. Do not practice it if you have even minor back problems.

2 Breathing out, turn your head to your left and let your knees slowly fall to your right. Try not to arch your back as you do this and drop your knees only as far as is comfortable.

3 Breathing out, turn your head to the right and let your knees fall to the left. Breathe in and return to the starting position to complete the set. Repeat the exercise 7–10 times.

WATCH OUT

Take your knees only as far as they will naturally go. Here, they have moved too far, causing the back to overarch and the pelvis to move out of neutral.

back **Turn**

Aim: To improve the turning capability of your spine along its entire length. Like the previous exercise, this helps to promote greater flexibility of movement and is good practice for keeping the pelvis in neutral and a good alignment as you turn.

head, neck, and spine in alignment

1 Kneel so that your knees are as close together as they will comfortably go and your buttocks are resting on your heels. Make sure that your pelvis is in the neutral position, gently pull in your abdominal muscles, and pull up on the pelvic floor.

SAFETY POINTS

• Stop if you feel any pain when performing this exercise. Again, clicks or pops that are not accompanied by pain are most likely to be caused by the release of pressure from the joints.

• Stop if you feel a tingling or pins-and-needles sensation in your face, hands, or feet.

• Move smoothly in and out of the final position and don't hold it, as this may cause cramps.

hands rest gently on the knees

2 Breathe in and turn slowly to your right, placing your right hand behind your back and your left hand on your right thigh as you turn. Keep turning until you reach a point of mild tension, then stop—be aware that you may not be able to look over your shoulder. Return to your original starting position as you breathe out.

3 Breathe in again and turn slowly to your left, placing your left hand behind your back and your right hand on your left thigh. Again, keep turning until you reach a point of tension, then slowly release the turn as you breathe out. This completes one set. Repeat this 7–10 times, keeping your movements slow and relaxed.

quadriceps and hip **Stretch**

Aim: To stretch and lengthen the quadriceps (thigh) muscles. The quadriceps travel over two joints—the hip and the knee joints. This exercise works to open up the front of the hip while gently bending the knee of the same leg. Involving both of the joints in this controlled way provides a safe and effective stretch and helps you to practice abdominal control.

EQUIPMENT: Large pillow.

back in line with
neck and head

pillow supporting
the head

knees bent to
90-degree angle

1 Lie on your left side, placing a pillow on your left arm and resting your head on it to keep your neck straight and relaxed. Your legs should be together and bent at the knees to about 90 degrees, or as close as you can comfortably come to it. Keep your back straight without locking it, gently draw your abdominal muscles toward your spine, and pull up on your pelvic floor. Breathe in widely and deeply.

SAFETY POINTS

• Avoid this exercise if you have weak knees, hips, or shoulders as it may exacerbate problems. Stop if any clicking or crunching occurs in your knee.

• You may experience a burning sensation in the front of your hip and along your thigh. This may be caused by stretching a nerve. Seek medical advice if you feel any pain during this exercise.

2 Breathe out and reach for the top of your right foot. Breathe in while holding your foot. Breathe out and gently pull the hand holding the foot toward the buttocks to stretch the front of the thigh. The stretch should be held as long as you are breathing out—the longer you can breathe out, the longer you can hold the stretch. You will be able to lengthen your breath with practice, so don't strain.

WATCH OUT

Making sure that you maintain abdominal control and a neutral pelvis position will help you to keep your back straight. Here control has been lost and the back is overarched.

3 Breathe in and gently release your hold on your foot, returning your leg to its original position. Gently roll over onto your right side, moving the pillow to support your neck. Check that your alignment is good and that you have retained a pelvic neutral position and good abdominal control. Now repeat the exercise on the left leg. This completes one set. Repeat the exercise 7–10 times.

thigh toner and calf **Stretch**

Aim: To lengthen the hamstrings and calf muscles, stretch the Achilles' tendons, and improve the quadricep muscles. The wall provides support for the spine so this is a good exercise if you have a weak back or minor back problem.

1 Begin with your back against the wall and your feet at a distance away from the wall that allows you to slide into a comfortable squat. Your feet should be hip-width apart, pointing forward and parallel to each other. Keep your neck and head in good alignment with your spine—this may mean that the back of your head is away from the wall. Gently try to bring your shoulders against the wall, going as close to the wall as you comfortably can. Breathe deeply into your back and the sides of the lower ribs to prepare for relaxed movement.

SAFETY POINTS

• Experiment to see how far away from the wall you should be. Make sure that your knees do not move in front of your ankles when you squat.

• Keep the sliding action of this exercise smooth and controlled. Losing control as you slide up the wall could cause thigh or knee injury.

• If you feel any pain, stop and seek medical advice.

arms hanging loosely down

feet parallel

3 Breathe in and gently slide back up the wall, keeping your abdominal and pelvic floor tone. Once you have reached the upright position, step away from the wall and walk on the spot for a few steps to release tension in your thighs. Return to the wall and repeat the exercise 7–10 times.

2 Breathe out, pulling in your abdominals and raising the pelvic floor. Continuing to breathe out, slide 8–12 inches down the wall or until you feel a comfortable tension. Keep your knees above your ankles to reduce any risk of knee damage. You can go down until your thighs are horizontal, but this is not recommended in the beginning. As you slide down, the stretch on your Achilles tendon and calf muscles increases and you may feel the urge to go up onto your toes. Keep your heels on the ground.

opening the lower back and aligning
the Pelvis

Aim: To reduce tension in the lower back and help to align the pelvis. Squeezing the thighs together reduces tension in the hip and back. It also increases the tone of the adductor muscles that run down the inside of the leg and attach to the front of the pubic bone. This exercise helps to balance these muscles, which will gently pull the pelvis into line over time.

EQUIPMENT: Two folded towels or small pillows.

1 Begin in the Relaxation Position with a pillow under your head to keep your neck straight and relaxed. Rest your arms comfortably by your sides and breathe deeply into your back and the sides of your lower ribs to prepare for the exercise. Gently bring your abdominal muscles toward your spine and increase the tone of your pelvic floor by raising the muscles gently upward.

SAFETY POINTS

• Seek medical advice before attempting this exercise if you have recently suffered a groin injury.

• You may feel or hear a click or pop in the middle of your pubic bone. If it hurts or clicks recurrently, seek advice from a medical professional.

• Do not use this exercise as rehabilitation unless you have been so advised by a medical professional.

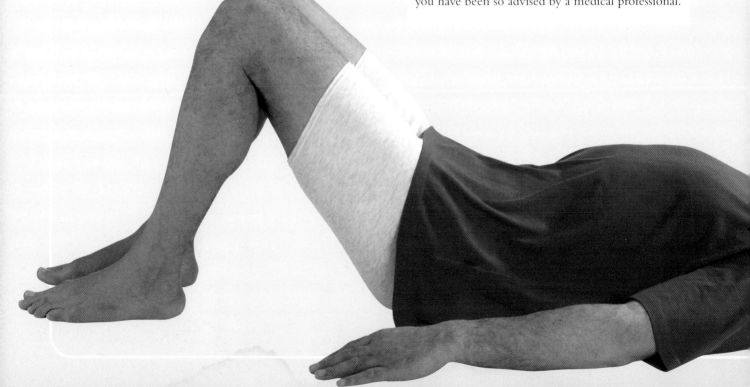

pelvis in neutral

chest relaxed

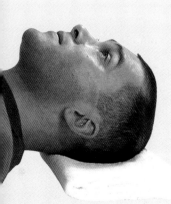

2 Place a pillow between your knees. Breathe out and gently squeeze your knees together. Be aware of any tendency to tense other areas of the body, such as the neck, chest, lower back, buttocks, or hips, as you breathe out. Try to keep a relaxed position and good body alignment throughout the exercise. Breathe in and then relax for a few seconds. This completes one set. Repeat 7–10 times.

WATCH OUT

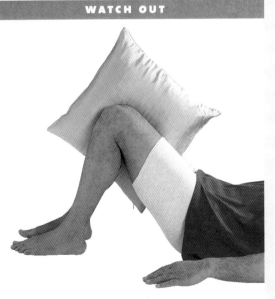

As you breathe out, try not to tense the hips or raise them off the floor. Focus your attention on keeping your pelvis in the neutral position.

ankle **Circles**

Aim: To tone the calf muscles, increase control, and improve the movement of the ankle joints. This is a good exercise to do at the end of a long day, particularly if you have been standing or walking a lot. It improves fluid drainage from the ankles, reducing puffiness. In addition, it can help to ease and reduce the ache or appearance of varicose veins.

ACTION NO.1

1 Begin in the Relaxation Position. Breathing out, engage your abdominals and pelvic floor muscles, bring your right knee up toward your chest, and clasp both hands around your thigh just above your knee. You may have one hand over the other or interlace your fingers. Make sure that you keep your head on the floor and stay in neutral pelvis.

ankle joints supple
and relaxed

knee brought up toward
the chest

shoulders kept relaxed
against the floor

2 Breathe in and slowly circle your ankle in a clockwise direction. Complete one full circle, then change direction, breathing out as you begin your counterclockwise movement. This is one set. Repeat this set 7–10 times on the right ankle, then repeat 7–10 times on your left ankle.

ACTION NO. 2

1 This is very similar to Action No. 1, giving you another way of improving the movement of your ankle joints. Breathe in widely and deeply and circle your right ankle in a clockwise direction. As you breathe out, move the ankle in a second clockwise circle. This completes one clockwise set. Repeat 7–10 times. Change the direction of the movement, but continue working the right ankle. Breathe in as you rotate the ankle in a counterclockwise direction, then breathe out as you rotate it again. This is one counterclockwise set. Repeat 7–10 times. Change ankles and repeat both sets on the left ankle.

SAFETY POINTS

• If you feel any pain in the joints or clicking or popping noises while doing this exercise, you should seek the advice of a medical professional.

• These two exercises are not suitable for use as forms of rehabilitation unless you have received professional medical advice beforehand.

ankle **Stretch**

Aim: To give a passive stretch to the ligaments and tendons around your ankle joint. Like the previous exercise, this will increase the flexibility of your ankle joints with time and practice. It also helps to tone up your calf muscles. As you can do it in a chair, it is an easy exercise to practice at any time, for example during a break at work.

EQUIPMENT: Chair, pillow or folded towel.

1 Sit on the floor—place a pillow or folded towel under your buttocks if you find this more comfortable—and stretch your legs out in front of you. Cross your right leg over your left leg, resting your right ankle on your left thigh.

SAFETY POINTS

• If you have tight hips, you may experience a tingling or pins-and-needles sensation in your foot. This is less likely to happen if you sit on a chair.

• If you feel or hear any clicking or cracking that is sharp or painful, stop and seek medical advice.

foot resting comfortably on thigh

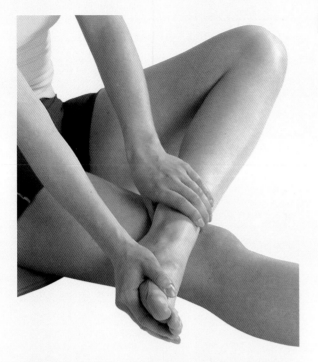

2 Support your foot by gently but firmly holding just above your right ankle with your right hand. Place your left palm on the sole of your right foot and use your thumb to hold the base of your right big toe. This provides stable support.

If you find it uncomfortable to sit on the floor, you can do this exercise sitting on a chair. Make sure that you maintain a neutral pelvis position.

3 Relax your ankle and circle it around with your left hand—the bigger and slower the circles, the better the stretch. Do 7–10 circles in one direction, then change direction and repeat 7–10 times. Change your foot and grip and repeat on the left side, circling the ankle 7–10 times in each direction. This makes one set. Repeat five times.

glossary

alignment The ideal relative positioning of the head, spine, and limbs for optimum movement efficiency, muscle control, and joint health

centering Using the muscles of the torso, predominantly the transversus abdominus, to provide stability and ease of movement in all exercises and daily activities

cervical lordosis A condition in which the top of the spine is distorted outward

coordination The ability to use various limbs at the same time, often combined with breathing exercises in Pilates

deltoids The muscles forming the rounded shape of the shoulders used for raising the arm

ectomorph One of the three body types, typified by a tall, thin frame and slow muscle growth

endomorph One of the three body types, typified by short, rounded build and protruding chest and stomach areas

fascia system The system of soft tissue that separates individual muscles from each other

flexibility One of the principal goals of Pilates exercising, to be able to move easily and gracefully in the full range of your body's unique potential

lateral breathing An efficient method of breathing in which the lungs expand to the side

latissimus dorsi The muscles situated on the ribs under the arms used for lowering the arms

lumbar lordosis A condition in which the lower spine is distorted forward

mesomorph One of the three body types, typified by an athletic build, large chest area, and tight stomach area

muscular system The body's means of movement and strength, the muscles hold the bones together. Muscle control is one of the key goals of Pilates

nervous system The body's network of sensory fibers, relaying messages to and from the brain

osteoporosis A condition in which the bones become porous due to lack of calcium

pectorals The muscles situated on the upper ribcage forming the chest

Pilates, Joseph The original creator of the Pilates approach to exercise and Pilates equipment, he was born in Germany in 1880 and died in the United States in 1967

posture The way the body is held when in a normal upright position. Pilates aims to improve posture by building muscle strength and alignment

quadriceps The muscles situated on the front of the thigh

relaxation position One of the key Pilates exercises in which the spine, hips, and limbs are held in optimum relaxation and the muscles at rest

skeletal system The body's frame of bones. Pilates aims to improve bone health

stabilization The condition in which the body is held in its optimum position and thus spine and limbs are stable

stamina The ability to perform prolonged physical exertion

thoracic kyphosis A condition in which the upper spine is distorted forward

thoracic straight spine A condition in which the upper spine looses its proper curve

transversus abdominus The muscles over the abdomen used in Pilates as the center of overall body control

visceroptosis The loss of abdominal muscle tone in which the stomach slouches forward and downward

well-being A state of overall health, fitness and contentment—a principal goal of Pilates

useful addresses & **Contacts**

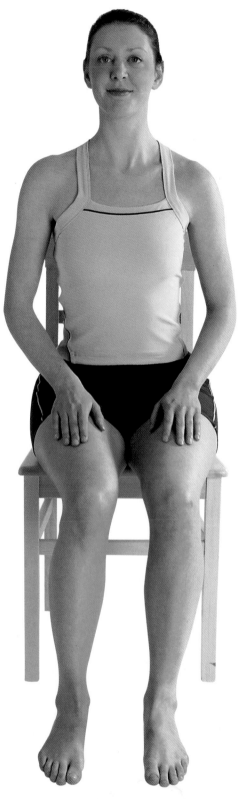

The Pilates Center

4800 Baseline Road, Suite D206

Boulder, CO 80303

Telephone: 303.494.3400

Fax: 303.494.5151

info@thepilatescenter.com

The Pilates Center of Austin

5555 N. Lamar Boulevard, Suite E103

Austin, Texas 78751

Telephone: 512.467.8009

info@pilatescenterofaustin.com

Alternative Health & Fitness Concepts

2016 Walnut Street, 2nd floor

Philadelphia, PA 19103

1-877-9Pilates

Telephone: 215.567.4969

Fax: 215.567.4881

pilatesbodyiq@mindspring.com

Balanced Body Inc

7500 14th Avenue #23

Sacramento, CA 95820

Telephone: 1.800.Pilates

www.balancedbody.com

Pilates Method Alliance

2631 Lincoln Avenue,

Miami, FL 33133

Telephone: 866.573.4945

www.pilatesmethodalliance.org

Body Balance

1009 North Rush Street, 4th floor

Chicago, IL 60611

Telephone: 312.440.9558

www.bodybalanceltd.com

Every Body Pilates

454 Common St. Belmont, MA 02478

Telephone: 617.484.3311

www.everybodypilates.com

index

a

age 8, 10, 11, 16

alignment 30–1, 54–5, 62–3,
    64–5, 66–7, 78–9

ankle
    circles 86–7
    stretch 88–9

arm opening 68–9

arms
    double light 40–1
    single light 38–9

b

back
    curls 74–5
    turn 78–9

backstroke, the 60–1

body type 22–3

brain 14

breathing 9, 24, 28
    lateral 52–3, 57
    relaxation position and 57

c

calf stretch 82–3

centering 24, 28

cervical lordosis 18

chest opening 68–9

chin tucks 66–7

circulation 8, 9

computer 8

coordination 24, 26, 60–1

cross over stretch 72–3

cycling 30

d

deltoids 44

diabetes 11

digestion 9

double light arms 40–1

e

ectomorph 22–3

endomorph 22–3

England 6

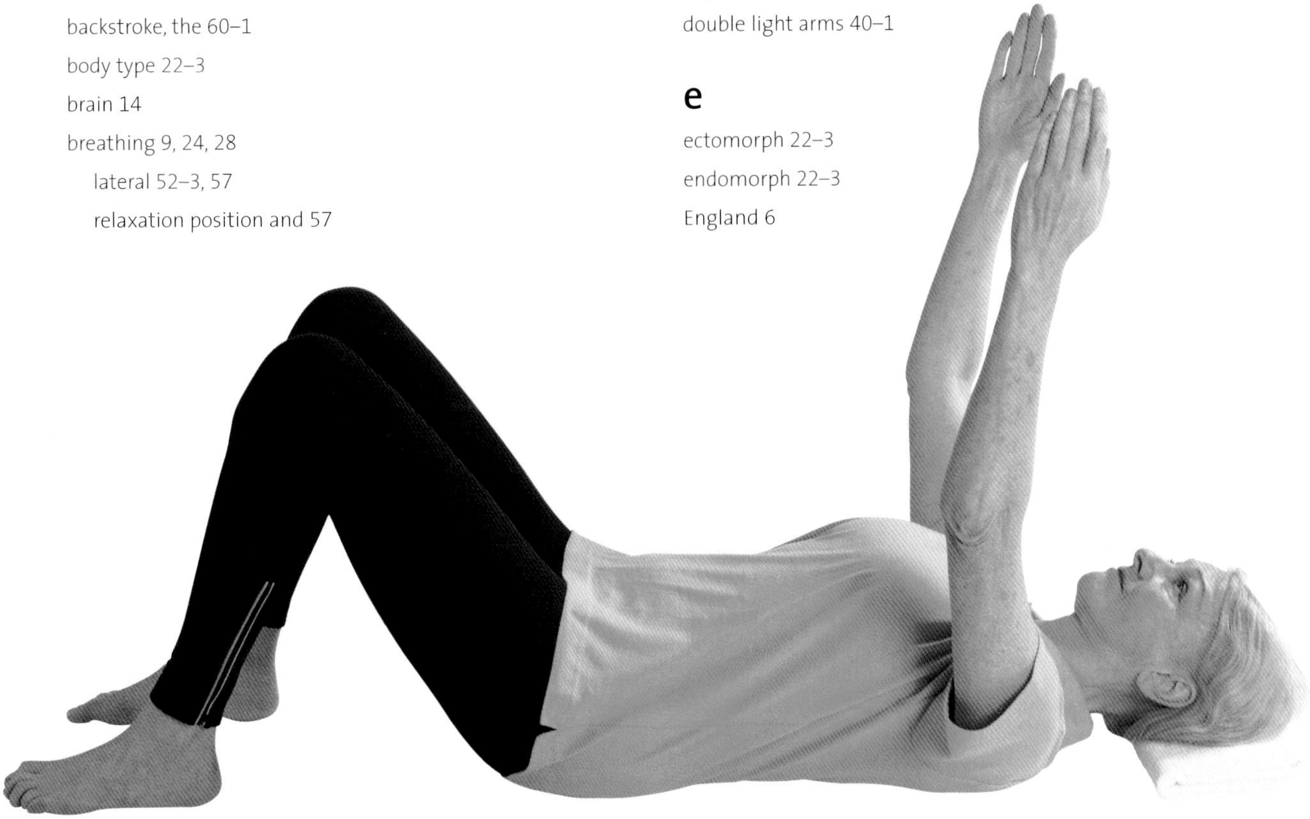

f

fascia system 14, 16

flexibility 9

g

glandular infections 11

h

health 10, 11

heart conditions 11

hip stretch 80–1

i

immune system 9

illnesses 10

influenza 11

irritable bowel syndrome 21

k

knees 19, 34–5, 42–3

kyphosis, thoracic 18

l

lateral breathing 52–3

lateral lunges 50–1

latissimus dorsi 44

legs, strong 42–3

light arms and strong legs 42–3

lordosis, cervical 18

lordosis, lumbar 18

low back, opening the 84–5

lower back turns 76–7

lumbar lordosis 18

lumbar spine 48, 50

m

medication 11

menopause 11

menstruation 11, 21

mental focus 24–5

mesomorph 22–3

muscle tone 8, 9

muscular system 11, 14, 15

n

nervous system 14, 15

neck

    rolls 64–5

    stretch 66–7

o

optimum relaxation 15

osteoporosis 16

overcontraction 15

overstretching 15

oxygen 9

p

pectorals 44

pelvic neutral 54–5

pelvis, aligning the 84–5

Pilates, Joseph 6, 24, 28, 32, 60

posture 6, 7, 16, 18–21

    sitting 46–7

pregnancy 10, 11

q

quadriceps 82–3

    stretch 80–1

r

relaxation 25

    position 56–7

    position and breathing 57

    position and stabilizing 58–9

s

safety 10–13

shoulder stretch 70–1, 72–3

single light arms 38–9

sitting posture 46–7

skeletal system 14, 17

skin 9

smooth movement 24, 26–7

spinal cord 14

stabilization 58–9, 62–3, 64–5, 66–7

stamina 24, 30

standing posture 34–7

straight spine, thoracic 18

strength 9

stress 9

swayback 18

swimming 30

t

thoracic kyphosis 18

thoracic straight spine 18

thigh toner 82–3

transversus abdominus 28

uvw

United States 6

Universal Reformer 6

upper body

    raises 44–5

    control 62–3

visceroptosis 18

waist turns 48–9

well-being 6, 8, 12

World War I 6

xyz

yoga 6

acknowledgments

The publishers would like to thank the
following for supplying props for photography:
The Pier, 200 Tottenham Court Road,
London W1P 0AD, England